# Promote the General Welfare

## Our Abused Constitution

By Steve Preston

2<sup>nd</sup> Edition

2018

# Contents

# Introduction

No matter what you believe, our Constitution has served to protect our freedoms better than any other in the entire world. Today, people a talking about elimination of freedoms [Socialism] to allow for increasing short term comfort just as many others did around the world and it always has caused a failure of society. Rather than a democracy that plays to majority rule and eventually plays into the hands of the greed of the wealthy, our founding fathers  developed a democratic republic with safeguards and control for everyone and reduction in the horrors of monopoly that are now being broken down by the power of companies like Amazon, Apple, Microsoft, Federal Research Bank, Lockheed Martin, and others. If we don't get back to basics; increase freedom over comfort and monopoly control over open competition, we will not long survive. I'm certain some of this book will make you angry, but we need to understand our government if we are to keep ourselves living and enjoying the freedoms of our peculiar society. Let's start with some basic definitions to get you fuming before expanding on how we got where we are and why these efforts have assured freedom.

**Inalienable Rights-** "*Rights given by the creator to those who worship him that no government can build laws around or restrict*". [Life, Liberty, Pursuit of happiness, self-protection, protection of one's property, equality of man by

God, and the right to bear arms to have protection against an overpowering government among others. By the way, if you have no belief in a creator, you probably should not assume you have inalienable rights of the God-fearing majority.

**Freedom** – Freedom is hard. You have the freedom to excel, work in the areas you desire and you have the freedom to starve if you want or go out in the desert with no water. Additionally, you have freedoms specifically spelled out to secure your Inalienable Rights, by God, that our government is or was not supposed to interfere with except as an arbiter between States.

**Freedom of Religion-** first off, religion means *"The belief in and worship of a superhuman controlling God"*- freedom of religion is the non-interference of government when you practice same. It is not a freedom to allow public bug-eating simply because you call it a religion. It is not a freedom to have sex with a dead person because you call it a religion.

**Freedom of speech-** This is the freedom to be punched in the nose for saying something offensive, but the government is not allowed to interfere with your freedom except to LIMIT harm that you may bring on yourself.

**Pursuit of Happiness-**Is not getting things, in fact it is the opposite. Pursuit of Happiness is an allowance or freedom to work hard to protect or advance your lifestyle without government hinderance and protection to allow you to work to limits which are set simply to reduce interference with someone else's pursuit of happiness. The Bible said it plainly in 2 *Thessalonians 3:10- "If any will not work, neither let him eat."*

**General Welfare-** This does not mean you are given stuff to keep you happy and alive. It means the country will assure the majority rule with protection of the weak. While the weak have a level of protection it is only to the limitation of the general consensus. If most think a man should marry a woman. Other deviations can be protected up to the point of hindering the majority.

**Pursuit of Happiness-** This does not mean that you can change the outward appearance of your sex and still retain your job. It simply means you can act with various deviations provided they don't hinder the morality of the Majority. It does not mean a mother can killed her unborn child as a means of birth control or reduction in the size of her family, or she did not want another boy without having to pay some type of payment for what she did to the baby unless the majority think this type of control is to be adopted and then those not doing it should have to pay.

I know those definitions are a little harsh and compassion must also be added into government by secondary law provided that a majority of legislators decide on those things and that is why we have a Congress. Again, let me say, I cannot assure you that everything in this book will be something you like, but many of the things are things you need to hear. Generally speaking, the book is about a small part of the Constitution that is so very important to repeat over and over. This would be our "third Constitution" and it tells us something special about how the government will be run. The main topic throughout the document is a seemingly simple requirement.

> *"To promote the General Welfare, and secure the Blessings of Liberty to ourselves and our Posterity".*

Liberty is not communism or democracy based it is something that must be worked on all the time and it requires something special that our Constitution carries called 'Inalienable Rights from God'. So long as the government understands there are limits to its power and those working for us in this government understand this concept, we will survive. This same sentiment was rooted in the founding fathers' documents from the very first "Union of Colonies" established in 1765 and is the cornerstone of our freedom, or country, and our prosperity.

The 1st Declaration of Independence [1765] simply said the following establishing the idea of liberty.

> *There are Essential Rights & Liberties of the Colonists*

Our 1st Constitution [1774] said a similar statement in a roundabout way.

> *To obtain redress which threaten destruction to the lives, liberty, and property of -subjects in North America- and the rights of freemen as inimical to the liberties of their country under the sacred ties of virtue, honor and love of our country*

Our 2nd Declaration of Independence [1776] said it more clearly as we began to understand the costs of both general welfare and liberty.

*Life, Liberty, and the Pursuit of Happiness were sacred and it was the duty of the government, to provide new guards for their future security.*

Our 2nd Constitution [1781] said it this way.

*The said "United States of America" enters into a firm league for their common defense, the security of their liberties, and their mutual and general welfare, binding themselves to assist each other, against all forces offered, on account of religion, sovereignty, trade, or any other pretense whatever. The free inhabitants of each of these States, paupers, vagabonds, and fugitives from justice excepted, shall be entitled to all privileges and immunities.*

This book deals mostly with the sentiment of "Promotion of general welfare and the pursuit of liberty for our Posterity". As it has been twisted in knots over the years to do everything from starting wars and almost to the destruction of our way of life, this simple phrase must continuously be reviewed and acknowledged or our nation will not long survive. To understand this short set of words, we need to start from the beginning to get a little background before we look at how to tell when our liberty and welfare are both being yanked away. The first part of the book deals in the lead up to our 3rd Constitution and how the words established in the first place tried to eliminate the horrors of slavery of all types. Today, it seems that people have a blind side to truth and understanding of what makes our nation great <u>because</u> of General Welfare and the Pursuit of Liberty.

These 2 ideals seem simple, but they only come at tremendous cost in focus, patriotism, understanding our government, and sometimes even life. Before we get into the meat of General Welfare and the Pursuit of Liberty, lets first go down memory lane an investigate times we were not using these 2 great concepts. Unfortunately it has happened a lot, but we somehow refocus on our Constitution enough to keep us a strong country---so far--- . For those who are not into American history too much and how we have established a governing document that is beyond any in the world let's look at the 5 documents that led to our current controlling document. There are 2 Declarations of Independence and 3 Constitutions we have used to build what we use today.

## Declarations of Independence against the UK

**"Declaration of Rights and Grievances"** [1765] under the <u>traitorous</u> President Timothy Riggles

**"Declaration of Independence"** [1776] under President John Hancock

## Constitutions of the Colonial/State Federations

**"Articles of Association"** [1774] under President Peyton Randolph

**"Articles of Confederation"** [1781] under President Samuel Huntington [our first Slave President-- Andrew Johnson would be our only other Slave President]

**"The Constitution"** [1789] under President George Washington

While all this was going on, let me give you a quick overview of the hardships of our country to hold on to our country and many would try to go around the elements of the Constitution and every time, disaster would ensue. We should start with George Washington. While there is no doubt he was a great man, his underhanded business dealings almost split the country apart.

## 1790 Washington Fiasco

If you were wondering how George Washington a fairly low-level farmer miraculously had a net worth of over $½ Billion in year 2000 dollars when he became President. He became the 2nd most wealthy President ever just barely behind John Hancock and now Donald Trump. The method used to legally steel the money isn't pretty and it caused the 2nd Civil War of our new Country. The 1st Civil War [1786] was fought for equal representation and the farmers lost as was the next 3 Civil Wars, but it is the second Civil War of 1894 that addresses George Washington's huge windfall as well as that of John Astor and Stephan Girard. All were land speculators, but during this time there was something very stinky.

An unusual law 'somehow' passed that placed a 28% tax on the production of whiskey and other farm related elements and devalued the American Currency to almost nothing. These things pushed land owners into bankruptcy. Farmer's started losing everything because of the worthless currency Influential "eastern land speculators" like George Washington bought the <u>worthless currency and land deeds</u> that were attached to farmer debt at pennies on the dollar. The government unbelievably purchased all the "worthless money" from the "fortunate land barons". This purchase came to **21 million dollars [over $½ Billion in year 2000 dollars].** Here is the sneaky part. After the money was in the hands of Washington, Astor, Girard and a few others, the <u>government bought the almost worthless money at the original face value</u>, which, in turn, greatly increased the value of the now easterner-owned land. This was such a good scheme that at least 3 of the richest men ever in America became wealthy beyond belief. In today's currency, their estates combined were worth $135 Billion. They are considered the 4th, 7th, and 50th richest men ever in the history of the United States before the year 2000 when everything went crazy. The horrible dismemberment of our Constitutional values almost destroyed us, but somehow, we survived as we began putting in place las to eliminate this type of evil from happening again---at least until the Federal Reserve began its lust for power. The following shows the ranking of these rich Americans who found or contrived this loophole.

| Rank | Land Baron | Birth/Death | Source of Wealth | Estate [$B] |
|------|------------|-------------|------------------|-------------|
| 4 | John Jacob Astor | 1763-1848 | Land in Penn. | 78 |
| 7 | Stephen Girard | 1750-1831 | Land in NY | 56 |
| 50 | G. Washington | 1732-1799 | Land in Virginia | 0.7 |

### 1860 Lincoln Fiasco

Most Americans know about Abraham Lincoln and the 4th Civil War he and the inappropriate representation by the Industrial States started and how 30 of the richest men ever in the history of the United States made fortunes off the horrors of the war, but how much was actually caused by Lincoln is not well understood as he probably was just a puppet for the most villainous people trying to do everything possible to take the wealth away from farmers. Within 5 years the entire country was on the brink of collapse, desperation, and massive poverty, as these 30 had control of most of the money in the country and we had turned into a Fascist State and most farmers lost all representation while the few Industrialists running the country without monopolistic restrictions were bleeding the country dry. For some unknow reason a miracle occurred and several anti-monopoly laws were initiated and a large number of these people simply started giving their ill-gotten gains away. Our Country began using our Constitution again and we would survive. Until speculation reared its ugly head.

## 1933 FED Fiasco

Without needed restrictions on speculation, we, again came to the brink of collapse as a huge Depression again ushered the horrors of an inappropriately regulated Republic that had wandered too far from the ideals of the Constitution; then came another horror. Our country slid into a mess that began in 1933 when the country went bankrupt and the debt was 'sort of' paid by something called the Federal Reserve Bank that is not part of the 'Federal' Government, does not hold a 'reserve' of money, and is not a 'bank'. This entity took up all our real money and reissues FRB IOUs with no basis of worth. Because they held control of money they were able to get the government to pass a new law that stated--

*Anyone who tries to pay for good using real money will be taxed 100% of the worth of the sale.*

The FED's control increased more and more and now a massive monetary correction is expected if we can remove their stranglehold.

## 1938-1945 War Fiasco

Wealthy Industrialists from UK and USA finance Hitler's War. These include Herriman, Bush, Ford, Standard Oil, and Rothchild's Banking even when they were apparently attacked by Hitler at the beginning of the war. The war made them all wealthier and with Hitler as an egotistical scapegoat, their treachery was not well understood until recently.

## 1947 CIA Fiasco

To help the Federal Reserve control the Government and new branch of Government called Central Intelligence Agency was adopted. Their main job was to expand the control of the FED by whatever means was needed. This included murder, blackmail, control of the media, and so many horrors most would not mention.

## Five Eyes Fiasco 1955

Why would the CIA and Federal Reserve want to do this you might be asking? The answer is to destroy the United States as an entity to allow for a one-world-government that would allow for easier control. To help in this plan something called 5-Eyes was established which linked the spying groups of UK, Canada, New Zealand, and Australia with the CIA of the United States as a spy ring that went beyond the <u>unnecessary description</u> of countries. Any citizen was now under the possible control of a worldwide agency with no scruples. Many politicians in these countries were soon under their control.

## Kennedy 1962 Speech

John F. Kennedy tells the world he will be disbanding the corrupt CIA. They had almost brought us into another worldwide war and Kennedy knew something had to be done or the United States could collapse.

## Kennedy 1963 Murder

From newly released documents it is apparent that CIA operatives killed Kennedy and CIA operative George HW Bush seen at the murder site.

Image on the right is of GHW Bush watching the Assassination or, at least at Dallas in some capacity for the CIA. Results of Johnson taking the Presidency is the Investigation and dismantling of the CIA was halted, but the CIA slowed down its massive desire to destroy the United States to build a new one world government but it did not stop them.

## Johnson Fiasco 1964

As Johnson was manipulated by this underbelly of our society, he adopted something called the "War on Poverty". This never was meant to reduce poverty but to establish poverty slaves that would be given a small amount of money if they could keep the right people in office to sustain the gift. While this almost destroyed the freedoms established by the Constitution it increased poverty massively and increase the control over the nations citizens.

## 1973 Operation Mockingbird

While the CIA had emplaced operatives in the Media since the early 1950s, in 1973 a full-scale attempt was initiated to take control of all media sources. By the early 1980s they had completed their objectives and set up Jewish controllers beholden to the CIA and FED controllers in 44 of the 45 news agencies used to provide news in the United States by 2016. I don't know why everything turns to a few Jewish families, but there is little evidence that does not show some close operational link between these groups. Some call it a Cabal, and others just call them dangerous. Fifteen billionaires currently own all the media and most are Jewish families. Of those 6 corporations actually control 96% of the media for the entire world, over $100 billion a year, so we are talking about a massive oligarchy.

**Levin/Time Warner** - TV and Movie [$32B]
**Eisner/Disney family**-TV and Movie [$23B]
**Bertelsmann**- News and Magazine [$16B]
**Redstone**/VIACOM/CBS- TV, Movie, Music[$14B]
**Murdoch**/Fox/NYTimes- TV and Movie [$13.5B]
**Messier**/Vivendi /Seagram- Phone, Film, Music [$10B]
Bronfmans, Newhouses, Sulzbergers, Zuckermans all play major roles

## 1989- 2009 Fake War Fiascos

The previous head of the corrupt CIA became president in 1989 [G.H.W. Bush]. This was followed by the corrupt Clintons and in 2001 who was followed by another corrupt G.W. Bush. We went to war while protecting those who fought against us, expanded the power of the CIA and the FED, we increased the drug trafficking of the CIA to support their attempt to reduce our sovereignty.

## 1990 Federal Reserve Fiasco

By 1990s all control of the Fed was from prominent Jewish families just like those families established in Operation Mockingbird and similar CIA initiated controls.

## 2010- 2016 American Apology Fiasco

Unbelievably, a man who had no past, strong affiliation with communists including his dad, and of the Moslem faith who represented those fighting against us in what we later found to be a fake war---- became President. No records of his birth, school, travels, were known and no history of politics or industrial management made it an impossibility for him to be elected except for the CIAs media, the CIA control of elections, the CIA control over congress and many who were blinded by the fact that he was only our 7th partially black President. He reduced our Military, made a global plea about the United States being horrible people. Then he allowed a massive terrorist worldwide war to escalate beyond anyone's imagination. He then reduced our border control and allowed for more immigration to water down American Ideals. He greatly increased the poverty in America and he began the expansion of communism in the United State to a level never seen before so that the Constitution could be replaced.

## Today

I don't know if we can reestablish our Constitution or not, but if we cannot we will fail as a nation just like Venezuela and other similar countries who trade in democratic republicanism for the horrors of communist/socialism.

One thing we need to do to protect our way of life is to reread our governing documents as detailed next.

# First Declaration of Independence 1765

The first Colonial Congress under President Timothy Ruggles had been a disaster. Our colonies had been united and established our first Declaration of Independence but the Traitorous President refused to sign the declaration. He stepped down as President and soon became a Colonel for the British opposition. With all the turmoil, the congress went home, but not until the Declaration had been issued.

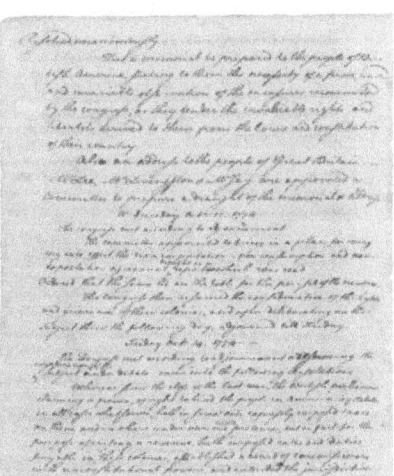
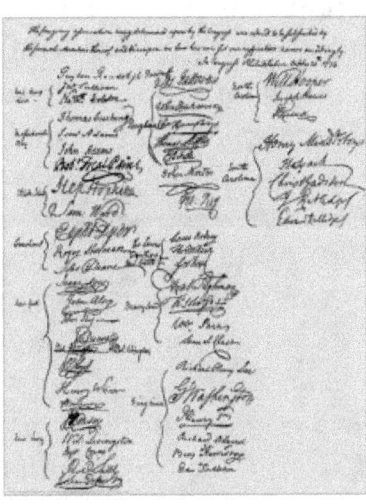

Claiming *"there are Essential Rights & Liberties of the Colonists"* the document went on to indicate this was manifested in requirements for trail by a jury, no taxation without representation and grievous acts limiting freedom allowed by all subjects. Then it listed what was required of them and their government to assure their liberty. It is amazing to me that the President of the United Colonies would not sign while everyone else began the steps to insure general welfare and the pursuit of liberty by taking the risks associated with freedom and building a model to assure the general welfare of what would soon be the United States of America. President Ruggles decided on the oppression of the 2nd class citizens as he was one of the elites. Soon he had established his place in the Tory Army as our country was thrust into war for freedom.

## Ruggles' Army

On 17 November, the main 'Loyal American Association' who would fight against freedom for the sake of comfort of the elite had formed its official command structure under the previous President of our new country, 'Timothy Ruggles'. Before becoming our first President, he had been a brigadier in the British controlled militia. Ruggles' orders to company captain Francis Green, dated two days before, give a sense of the group's duties.

*I have it in command to acquaint you, that the General expects (for the present) you take charge of the District about Liberty Tree & the Lanes, Alleys & Wharves adjacent, & that by a constant patrolling party from sunset, to sunrise you prevent all disorders within the district by either Signals, Fires, Thieves, Robbers, house breakers or Rioters.*

Within a short time, this same group became the Loyal American Regiment to continue their siege to remove even more freedom from Our north American society. Newspapers asked for volunteers in this war between Tories and Rebels, as shown below.

## Harvard Pilgrims Head the Tory Army

Here we go with the Pirates known as Pilgrims that is a different story]. The Tory invasion including Timothy Ruggles and other descendants of Pilgrims including Edward Winslow, Peregrine White, Resolved White and Richard Warren. All were what you could call descendent "traitors" and they were educated at Harvard, the breeding ground for those who hated freedom that would take away their power. Below is the ad to get soldiers to fight against the American "Rebels" by the man who had, for a short period of time, been President.

*All GENTLEMEN VOLUNTEERS,*
Who are willing to serve his Majesty in the
LOYAL AMERICAN REGIMENT
Commanded by
*Col. BEVERLEY ROBINSON,*
For TWO YEARS, or during the Rebellion, shall upon their being mustered and approved of by the Inspector-General, receive
*Twenty-five Dollars Bounty.*
Whatever Persons are willing to embrace the present Opportunity offered or approving their Loyalty, let them repair to the Quarters of the Regiment, at Haerlem, Heights, or to the Bull's Head Tavern, at New-York, where an Officer will attend to receive and entertain them.

### Rewarded for his Crimes

By 1775, our traitor President left Boston for Nova Scotia with the British troops and accompanied Lord Howe to Staten Island. His estates were confiscated, and in 1779 he received a grant of 10,000 acres of land in Nova Scotia by the British Government. He settled there along with a lot of money for his Traitorness. Don't even consider this guy as a President at all. I don't!

# 1st Constitution [1774]

It would not be until the 2nd Colonial Congress came into being under President Peyton Randolph. Riggles was gone into hiding by this time and the Union of American Colonists began to take steps to understand what General Welfare and the pursuit of liberty would be for them. The first Constitution called the **Articles of Association** did not call out many of the detailed specifications for governing beyond the elimination of slavery, halting the purchase of tea, and limitations concerning how many pimentos one was allowed to eat, but it certainly was a start to show the cost of freedom and general welfare. There would be a level of suffering that would allow these things to happen. People knew it and set up rules and processes to achieve them. Below is a complete copy of our first Constitution.

**A Second President**-It was President Randolph's time. Ten years had passed, the British were even more oppressive than they had been before the first Declaration of Independence, and the population was more strongly convinced that there was a price to pay for <u>general welfare and the pursuit of liberty.</u> No one was going to get a free lunch, no one was going to be given special consideration and all had to participate or they would be shunned by those fighting for a continuation of general welfare. This was becoming a democratic environment set up with all having to take part or leave. While the Constitution they established was fairly loose in design, our President proudly signed the document putting a target on his head along with others in the Congress. Even at this early date in 1774, there was not only a strong feeling for promoting the <u>General Welfare and Freedom,</u> there was also a strong desire to expand our United Colonies from the current 11 colonies. The desired goal included a split of Pennsylvania into the religious sector and a more liberal section now called Delaware who wanted to keep slavery and drinking alive, Georgia who was finally coming on board, Canada who had been asked to join the United Colonies over the last ten years, and the simple takeover of all the land called <u>Vandalia</u> that had been sort of given to the Indians against the wishes of the colonists. [We will look at this in more detail later.] They hated the violence of the Indians and would refer to them as savages in the new Constitution. By declaration our country would be doubled in size even with Canada rejecting the invitation and Americans would learn what **promoting the General Welfare and Freedom would cost**.

## A Crazy Constitution

This would be a crazy constitution. After our first "Declaration of Independence" [Declaration of Rights and Grievances]" this first Constitution would change the colonies into a nation with  the rights and duties of a nation. Let's review this important document to compare characteristics with our 3rd Constitution we are using now. Certainly, there was a flavor of British rule acceptance, but we can tell the union was now thinking like a separate country.

## But just what did our first Constitution say?

It starts off innocuous enough with praise to our big brother Britain and sort of vowing allegiance only to turn around and begin an attack on the oppression, the enslavement, and the ruinous nature of the British rule--- to go along with the Declaration of Independence that had been sent.

### Praise and Anguish Paraphrased

We, his majesty's *most loyal subjects, the delegates of the several colonies of New Hampshire, Massachusetts Bay, Rhode Island, Connecticut, New York, New Jersey, Pennsylvania, the three lower counties of New Castle, Kent and Sussex, on Delaware, Maryland, Virginia, North Carolina, and South Carolina, deputed to represent them in a continental Congress-- are oppressed; -- occasioned by a ruinous system of colony administration, -- calculated for enslaving these colonies,*

Please notice Georgia was excluded in the original colonies of the union.

### Trade Refusal

*In North America, we are of opinion, that a non-importation, non-consumption, and non-exportation agreement, will prove the most effectual as follows:*

- *Article 1- Law against buying Pimento*
- *Article 2- Law against buying slaves*
- *Article 3- Law to halt drinking of Tea*
- *Article 4- Law to delay constitutional action*
- *Article 5- Law against foreign Merchant Piracy*
- *Article 6- Law against domestic Merchant Piracy*
- *Article 7- Law to produce domestic sheep*
- *Article 8- Law against wearing Scarves at funerals*
- *Article 9- Law against price gouging*
- *Article 10- Establishment of Welfare for Bostonians*
- *Article 11- Law against Treason*
- *Article 12- Law of Inspection*
- *Article 13- Price Control Law*
- *Article 12- Federal control over inter-colony trade and commerce*

### Call for the repeal of the following:

- *No trial by jury being carried out*
- *Law against blocking Boston harbor*
- *Law against altering the Boston charter*
- *Law to extend the limits of Quebec*

While one would think the book would discuss the welfare of the Bostonians clause, but what we will look at a little later is the discussion about freeing the slaves and how it affected the General Welfare described in the 3rd Constitution we use now. First, we need to get into a war. Soon the country was at war in the area known as Vandalia.

# Vandalia Battle that Started the Revolution

To understand this section, we must learn about the Western part of Pennsylvania call **Transylvania** by the colonists and **Indiana** by those who were trying to establish an Indian Trading colony. the land now called West Virginia called **Vandalia** by the British Government and **Ken-tu-Kee** by the Indians that hunted there. Americans were going to get a taste of the requirements for the "General Welfare and the pursuit of liberty".

While Randolph was President the War for Independence started in these two regions, Transylvania and Ken-tu-Kee. Remember I said, the Colonies had decided that the Indian colony of Vandalia [including Transylvania] should not be given to the savages that were in America and killing settlers. The united colonies under its new President knew it should be taken over by the other colonies. Well, here was one of the first tests of that resolve. It is known as the **Battle of Point Pleasant** and also the **Battle of Kanawha** in some older accounts. The battle occurred on October 10, 1774, primarily between Virginia "rebel" militia and American Indians or should I say the Vandalia militia made up of the Shawnee and Mingo tribes. Along the Ohio River near modern Point Pleasant, West Virginia, American Indians under the Shawnee **Chief Cornstalk** fought for their colony. [Isn't it strange to find such a strong Indian with such a weak name? Give me Stone, or Mountain, or Wolf over Cornstalk any day.] Sorry for the rambling. Anyway, they attacked Virginia militia of about

1000 men under Colonel Andrew Lewis, hoping to halt Lewis's advance into the Ohio Country to secure claim to the "newly identified land". After a long and furious battle, Cornstalk retreated. One could say this was one of the first victories of the Revolution, as the battles of <u>Lexington and Concord were fought in April 1775</u>. As I said, Peyton Randolph was President of the colonial union during this important battle that is usually ignored. After the Revolution, the country took control of all the land East of the Mississippi including all of Vandalia and Transylvania. The image following shows our original united colonies and the size we represented in our second Declaration of Independence. Our newest additions were New Hampshire, Georgia, and the colony of Vandalia that was split among the various colonies. It would be after the Revolution before the country of Vermont decided to become part of the United States to fill in a small hole between N.H. and the 'Maine' part of Massachusetts.

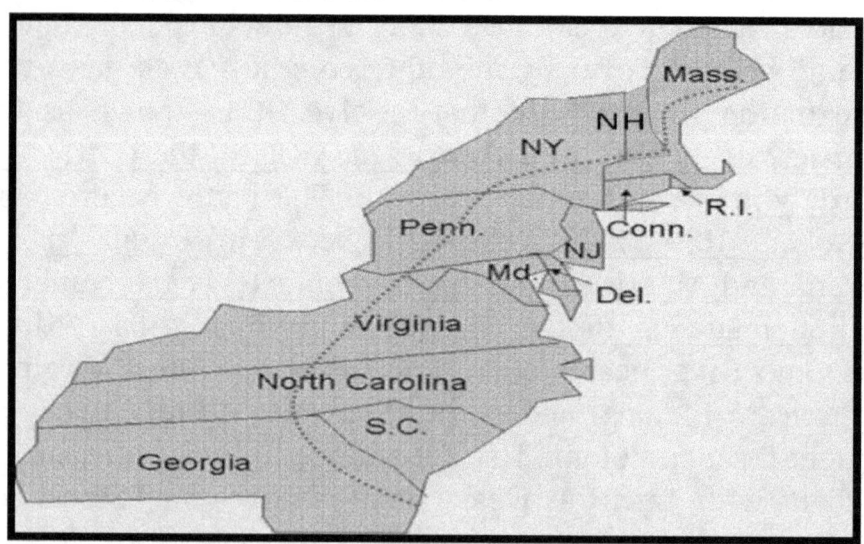

# Elimination of Micro-colonies and Slavery

General welfare would require similar say in our government. The early founding fathers knew of the issues of the micro-colonies and how their representation in Congress was substantially more that the "normal sized" States, so there was a campaign. Some may not have been told this in school, but I think it is important. While <u>Rhode Island, Connecticut, Delaware, and New Hampshire were split into micro-States again at a later time; during the time of the "Sons of Liberty" up until at least 1774, they were all piled into one colony and the flag had only 9 stripes</u> representing North and South Carolina, Virginia, New York, New Jersey, Pennsylvania, Massachusetts [including Maine], and the **North East micro-colonies** [including Connecticut, Delaware, Rhode Island, New Hampshire] as shown below.

Their snake flag went even farther making a reasonable State by adding Massachusetts to the North East microcolony set. The "Sons of Liberty" warned that if the Colonies did not join together they would soon die, as shown on the snake flag to the left. I guess the fear tactics worked as we soon would declare our Independence in a stronger way. They also warned of consolidation or unrest would be certain. This warning went unanswered. One of the campaign warnings of these courageous people beginning to fill the groundwork for our Constitution was to establish all Americans as individuals with all having liberty. Because of the massive conviction of John Jay who would soon become President and others, our new country would eliminate slavery. This attempt was focused mostly on indentured slaves of the North, but would soon be tried in the south where black slaves were becoming a major commodity. Let's look at the elimination of slavery article.

## Article 2 Elimination of Slavery

*We will neither import nor purchase, any slave imported after the first day of December next; after which time, we will wholly discontinue the slave trade, and will neither be concerned in it ourselves, nor will we hire our vessels, nor sell our commodities or manufactures to those who are concerned in it.*

To many this stand against slavery sounds odd given the harsh words in our second Constitution and the details about slaves only being 3/5 of a person as identified in the 3rd and final Constitution, but there is a story to tell.

# Slavery in America

This is not a book specifically on slavery or the hatred that ensured because of this horrendous custom, but many have gotten this whole thing mixed up and certainly slavery did affect the whole concept of **General Welfare and pursuit of liberty** so we cannot ignore it. The colonists and many regions of the British Empire began to be flooded with a new commodity throughout the 17th century. This commodity was slaves. John Jay and many of the founding Fathers made strong strides in eliminating the custom even before the American Revolution. By the time the 1st Constitution came about Slavery had been eliminated but that is not the whole story as we try to envision the moral requirements for -- *"Promoting the General Welfare and assuring Liberty for our Posterity."*

While it began its fast rise to popularity in early 17th century America, we will find it continued until the time of Thomas Jefferson when importing slaves was outlawed under our 3rd Constitution in 1808. They were shackled, whipped, hung, dragged, and beaten into submission. If they tried to escape, they were hunted down and killed. No! I'm not talking about the black slaves; I'm talking about the white ones. The British continued to supply this commodity into the new world as they tried to "cleanse" their precious United Kingdom. When white slavery is acknowledged as having existed in America, it is almost always termed as "temporary indentured servitude" or part of the convict trade, by the way, there were not many in the temporary column. The "convicts" transported to America under the 1723 Waltham Act, perhaps numbered 100,000. [Don't call them Slaves, but almost none became free in the land of the free!] To put this in perspective, the ENTIRE quantity of black slaves brought to the colonies over the entire 450 years of slave traffic, only 500 thousand. While the numbers are not accurately known, it is believed about 1.5 times that many criminals, indentured, and previously purchased white slaves were brought into the colonies over a much shorter timeframe. In the 1790 census there were about half a million slaves total in the United States. This would include Black, Indian, and White as Chinese slaves had not yet entered the new nation. At least ½ of the slaves would have been white from the huge influx from the UK.

| | 1790 [Million] | 1800 [M] | 1840[M] |
|---|---|---|---|
| Slaves * | 0.55 | 1.0 | 2.4 |
| Free | 3.5 | 5.6 | 14.6 |
| Total in USA | 4 | 6.6 | 17 |

*These are black and white slaves [no separation is provided in the census between indentured, prisoner, purchased or bred, white or black slaves. By 1840, the majority of slaves were black.]*

The major use of white slaves began to reduce substantially in the 18th century, there were still white indentured slaves coming to America into the beginning of the 19th century. From Jay and other anti-slavery protester, *"Promoting the General Welfare and assuring Liberty for our Posterity"* could only be accomplished if all slaves could be part of the society. As I mentioned this would have included black men, but most of the slaves the Jay had come in contact with were the slave factory workers in the northern States.

## Cavanaugh on Irish Slaves

According to James Cavanaugh, author of *Irish Slaves of the Caribbean*, the <u>English sold more Irish slaves between 1600 and 1699</u> than they did African slaves. **They were cheaper**, easier to offload, and <u>ordered by the government</u>. Cavanaugh indicated, *"The Proclamation of 1625 ordered that ALL Irish political prisoners be transported overseas and sold as "laborers" to English planters, who were settling the islands of the West Indies, officially establishing a policy that was to continue for two centuries. In 1629, a large group of Irish men and <u>women</u> were sent to Guiana, and by 1632, Irish were the <u>main slaves</u> sold to Antigua and Montserrat in the West Indies. But there were <u>not enough political prisoners to supply the demand</u>, so every petty infraction carried a sentence of transporting, and <u>slaver gangs combed the country sides to kidnap</u> enough people to fill out their quotas. In 1649, Cromwell landed in Ireland and attacked Drogheda, slaughtering some 30,000 Irish living in the city. Cromwell reported: 'I do not think 30 of their whole number escaped with their lives. <u>Those that did are in safe custody in the Barbados.</u>"* I know this depiction is of those sold in the Islands below the colonies, but many also were sold to the other British colonies of the region. Shock of shocks! -----A few months later, in 1650, 25,000 Irish were sold in the Americas. Typical victims are shown below left.

**White Child Slaves-**During the 1650s decade of Cromwell's Reign of Terror, over <u>100,000 Irish children</u> were taken from Catholic parents and sold as slaves in the New Americas. [See above right] Tens of thousands of the White slaves were kidnapped children.  To give you a feeling about the fear of your child being taken let's look at "English". The origin of the word "kidnapped" is kid-nabbed, the stealing of White children for enslavement. <u>The center of the trade in child-slaves was in the port cities of Britain and Scotland.</u> Many of the kid-nabbings were done by what were called "Press Gangs".

**Kid-Nabbing-**This segment comes from "Bound Over" by Van der Zee.  *"**Press gangs** in the hire of local merchants roamed the streets, seizing 'by force such boys as seemed proper subjects for the slave trade.' Children were driven **in flocks** through the town and confined for shipment in barns...So flagrant was the practice that people in the countryside about Aberdeen avoided bringing children into the city for fear they might be stolen; and so widespread was the collusion of merchants, shippers, suppliers and even magistrates that the man who exposed it was forced to recant and run out of town."*  Once the children were in the new world, some went to the factories as shown below.

The indentured servants, who served a tidy little period of 7 years polishing the master's silver and china and then taking their place in colonial high society, were a minuscule fraction of the great unsung hundreds of thousands of White slaves who were worked to death in this country from the early 17th century onward. Up to one-half of all the initial arrivals in the American colonies were white slaves and they were America's first slaves. These figures tell us that the 1$^{st}$ Constitution elimination of Slavery was to mostly halt white slavery. These white humans were almost always slaves for life, long before black Africans became more prominent. This slavery was even hereditary. White children born to White slaves were enslaved too. Whites were auctioned on the block with children sold and separated from their parents and wives sold and separated from their husbands. Free black property owners were on the streets of northern and southern American cities while White slaves were worked to death in the sugar mills of Barbados and Jamaica and the plantations of Virginia, so let's not forget that slavery was awful no matter what color someone happened to be.

It has been estimated that ninety percent of the White slavery in America was conducted without indentures of any kind but according to the so-called "custom of the country". Many places in the North American colonies, the custom was almost always continued servitude after the indenture. During the 1650s, <u>over 100,000 Irish children</u> between the ages of 10 and 14 were taken from their parents and sold as slaves in the West Indies, Virginia and New England. In 1656, Cromwell ordered that 2,000 Irish children be taken to the Americas and sold as slaves to English settlers. During this same time, 52,000 Irish (<u>mostly women and children</u>) were sold to Barbados and Virginia. Another 30,000 Irish men and women were also transported and sold to the highest bidder. You can imagine why so many women were among those sold. <u>There is no doubt that in 17th century colonial America and on both sides of the Atlantic, white slavery was a far more extensive operation than Black enslavement</u>. In the beginning of the 18th century, there were more white slaves and in the later part there were beginning to be a higher percentage of black slaves. <u>Even during the latter part of the 18th century there was kidnapping of Anglo-Saxons into slavery as well as convict slavery.</u>

**Proclamation of 1625**-The Irish slave trade began when James II sold 30,000 Irish prisoners as slaves to the New World. His Proclamation of 1625 required Irish political prisoners be sent overseas and sold to English settlers in the West Indies. <u>By the mid-1600s, the Irish were the main slaves sold to Antigua and Montserrat. At that time, 70% of the total population of Montserrat were Irish slaves</u>. Ireland quickly became the ***biggest source of human livestock*** for English merchants. Again, let me say it once more; the majority of the early slaves to the New World were white. Irish were the main country of export, initially because of religion and then simply because they were not considered human. From 1641 to 1652, <u>over 500,000 Irish were killed by the English and another 300,000 were sold as slaves.</u>

Ireland's population fell from about <u>1,500,000 to 600,000 in</u> <u>one single decade</u>. Before we could begin to eliminate the new push for black slaves, the trade of white slaves had to be eliminated. I know this is not a fair statement, but it provides the sentiment of the Revolutionaries. They did not turn around in the 2$^{nd}$ Constitution and want slavery again, they simply had changed focus on eliminating ALL slaves and it would be an uphill battle. Let's review a little about black slaves. While most know more of this segment, we still should address it as it was a horrible custom.

# Black Slavery

While we are talking about slavery, many already know white people were not the only slaves in America. We had better look at the cause of General Welfare and Pursuit of liberty when it comes to the black slave populations that would soon overtake the White slaves. **Black slavery was much worse in its devaluing of humanity**. While Andrew Johnson was able to bring himself up from white slavery to become President and possible Samuel Huntington did a similar unbelievable task, no black Chinese or American Indian Slaves Every were able to even be considered for the position. These non-white slaves were considered to be less civilized and even less human. Here are just a few of the examples from Abraham Lincoln, the Supreme Court, and 13th Amendment to the Constitution that was replaced after the 4th Civil War that show this horrible sentiment.

### Supreme Court Decision [1857]

*"The question before us is, whether [Negroes] ... compose a portion of [the American] people and are constituent members of this sovereignty? We think they are not.... On the contrary, they [are] ... **a subordinate and inferior class of beings**, who [have] been subjugated by the dominant race.... [They] can therefore claim none of the rights and privileges which [the Constitution] provides for ... citizens of the United States."*

## Senator Abraham Lincoln Address [1858]

*"I will say then that I am not, nor ever have been, in favor of bringing about in any way the **social and political equality of the white and black races.** I am not, nor ever have been, in favor of making **voters or jurors of Negroes, nor of qualifying them to hold office**, nor to **intermarry with white people.** I will say in addition to this that there is a physical difference between the white and black races which I believe will forever forbid the **two races living together on terms of social and political equality.** And inasmuch as they cannot so live, while they do remain together there must be the position of superior and inferior, and I as much as any other man am in favor of having **the superior position assigned to the white race.***

## Corwin's 13th Amendment [1861]

This amendment was pushed by Lincoln, and passed both houses and had already been ratified by a few States as the 4th Civil War of our country began. Here is the sentiment of the Nation.

*No amendment shall be made to the Constitution which will authorize or give to Congress the power to abolish or interfere, within any State, with the domestic institutions thereof, including that of persons held to labor or service by the laws of said State."*

As I mentioned before, the English and French black slave trade occurred between 1450 and 1900. While the yearly number of black slaves purchased in the colonies was fairly low, one can see from the sentiment of the nation that their lot was horrible. If you are wondering just how many Black slave POWs were exported from Africa, during this 450-year period there were <u>over 11 Million Africans</u> that were transported around the world. Here's the part to remember with respect to American History. <u>Only 4% of them were sold to the colonists</u> that would soon be called the United States. The rest found their way to other, not so pleasant, areas. It seemed like Africans were trying to destroy Africa during this terrible age. Just as one group would win one war and take away slaves, another group would beat the winning group and they would become slaves themselves. This was the African form of genocide and it was substantially different that Hitler's. Instead of killing the losers, the winners made money with them and still accomplished the same genocide. There was no reason to have huge prisons or even huge execution areas. This slave thing made warring easy and efficient. The groups that made out the most from the Africans killing each other and driving each other into slavery were the English and the French.

**Outlawed in 1808-**Only 500 thousand African slaves were brought to the United States colonies over the entire 450 years of the African slave trade. All the rest were born in the United States. <u>President Jefferson had outlawed the practice of receiving slaves from another country in 1808 </u>so most of the depictions of slave-ships continually coming to North America carrying sardine packed slaves is not a complete picture. The percentage of white and black slaves to non-slaves was continuously decreasing in the United States before the United States' 4th Civil War of 1862. As shown below, the slave population was <u>18% of the total population in 1800</u> [not including those classified as

41

indentured servants] and the percentage had dropped to only 13% by 1860.

| Slave Use Growth | 1800 | 1810 | 1840 | 1860 |
|---|---|---|---|---|
| Slaves north [M] | .2 | .2 | .4 | .4 |
| Free north [M] | 3 | 3.8 | 9.6 | 20.3 |
| Slaves south [M] | .7 | .9 | 2 | 3.2 |
| Free south [M] | 1.2 | 1.8 | 5 | 7 |
| % slaves north | 6% | 6% | 4% | 2% |
| % slaves south | 35% | 33% | 30% | 31% |

For those thinking the North and South ideals were substantially different we should note that the drop was about the same in both north and south with about a 4% drop in percentage of slave population experienced in both the north and south during this period. Certainly, there were more slaves in the Agrarian sections of the country, but the thing to look at here was that the numbers were going down. According to the 1860 census, there were over 130 thousand free black Americans living in the various "rebellion" States before the war started [about 3.5% of the black population]. While that number is appallingly low, it was getting larger every year as slavery was becoming a thing of the past. Here is a question, what State outlawed slavery first? You guessed it Georgia was the first to outlaw it in 1733, but the law was repealed within a year when the crops needed to come in, I suppose. By events of the war and normal consequence, black slavery eventually ended, but it still would take a long time for black Americans to be given the same consideration as white Americans. During the 1904 World's Fair a number of African exhibits showed the backwardness and less than civilized nature of the Africans and many Americans came to view this type of zoo as shown below left.

That brings us to the African pigmy named Ota Benga shown right. In 1906 he is well known as being the last African placed on display at the Bronx Zoo as the missing link. To add effect, Ota had a chimpanzee that he would carry and a small bow and arrow which he used to shoot at visitors. Finally, black Americans began feeling the freedoms of other Americans, but something called the "War on Poverty" would almost destroy that freedom. Right now, let's continue with another slave population. This one was not freed with the Emancipation Proclamation.

# Yellow Slavery

California was an important State for a number of reasons. Not only was San Francisco becoming one of the largest towns in the country, but more importantly, a new breed of slaves was erupting that would begin to weaken the control of the Industrialist States if nothing was done. These "slaves" were from China and they were unique. They worked harder than black slaves and they were NOT CALLED slaves. Certainly, they were beaten if they ran off, were segregated from Normal Americans, were required to work longer hours than normal people, were not allowed to marry and have children, were not allowed to own land, and were not allowed to stake a claim for gold or minerals, but they were sort-of paid for their services [less than a third of a Normal person] so no one had to say they were slaves. Anyone with half a brain would have recognized that this new type of slave would soon be instituted and the "slave substitute" in the slave States to increase production and to eliminate the slave stigma. If that happened, the mid-western agrarian States would not be able to be controlled by the Industrialist statettes [super tiny States that still got exactly the same number of Senators as a normal or huge State] and larger States in Congress as farmers would vote with farmers if the slave issue had been settled.

By far the major reason that black slave laborers were not the primary method for establishing the transcontinental Railroad was the Chinese labor force. The main reason that California had no "black" slaves and became a "free state" was this very same super cheap, beat-me, abuse-me labor force. They worked for practically nothing, worked harder than almost any slave, they complained less, and the typically didn't talk to anyone outside their own community. Who needed slaves with Chinese around? By 1860, almost 10% of the population of California was Chinese "quasi-slave-workers".

**Chinese Were <u>not</u> Slaves-**While we are on this subject that I'm staying out of let me say that the thousands of Chinese working on the railroad systems were in no way slaves. Yes, they were <u>whipped</u> if they tried to leave the railroad site and the <u>white workers of the railroads were paid about 300% times the average Chinese "salary"</u>. But that doesn't mean anything. Oh yes, the white workers on the railroads had box car housing while the "non-slave" Chinese had to <u>survive in tents or nothing</u> at all and these same Chinese were <u>considered to be less than human</u>. All this can be twisted out of proportion. After all, <u>the employers were the ones who were championing "anti-slavery"</u>. The images show the whipping, working without shoes, and tent housing in extremely cold snow conditions. Don't even think they were enslaved. Ha!

So, the question might be how did farmers exist after the Civil War? Well they used slaves of course, but they had more efficient ones in the form of Chinese. After the Emancipation Proclamation, Chinese rushed to fill the worker spots as <u>unfortunate black Americans now had no place to go</u>. Chinese in droves went to Arkansas and Louisiana, to work on plantations. Almost immediately after the Civil Right Act of 1870, the <u>Chinese gained the freedom of marriage</u>. The 1870 U.S. census of Louisiana showed a massive marrying rush with well over ½ of all Chinese marriages to black women so there was some carryover of black slavery, I suppose.

Initially entering the United States in the 1790s, once they got here they became <u>the new version of Slave in California</u>. By 1880, there were still well over 300 thousand Chinese still in California even with horrible treatment that left many dead. Here are some of the basic characteristics of this new commodity, that we shall not call slaves.

*They were classified as sub-human* and not allowed the services of the law hold office or even be on a jury [see below]

*They could not own land and could not become citizens*

*They could not marry white women* [Naturalization Act 1790 and Anti-Miscegenation Laws]

*Laws were passed to exclude Chinese immigration of women* that could increase the control of the Chinese and make their lives less burdensome. [Chinese Exclusion Act and Geary Act- not eliminated until 1924]

*They were [usually] paid a small amount [1/10th* of the "Normal" workers] by railroads, and consisted of 90% of the Worker/slave base. Beaten, chained, and not provided any housing, they were killed by the dozens in landslides, and explosions as they were forced to punch holes through mountainsides, but they still were paid so the 13th Amendment was not violated exactly.

*They had to pay "special taxes of $3 per day* under the "Foreign Miners Tax Act" if they wished to dig for minerals. [Average money obtained was $6 per month- Many fake tax collectors came collected additional tax, burned settlements, and drove Chinese away from mines without and redress by the law. This law lasted until 1870.]

### Chinese and the Supreme Court

This was before the Dred Scot decision that black slaves were not Americans. In 1854 the California Supreme Court, decided, the Chinese were sub human [Slaves] with no legal rights. Let's see what they said.

47

*They are-- a race of people whom nature has marked as inferior, and who **are incapable of progress or intellectual development** beyond a certain point, as their history has shown; **differing in color, and physical conformation**; between whom and ourselves nature has placed an impassable difference and as such had **no right to swear** away the life of a citizen or participate with us in administering the affairs of our Government. "*

These slaves were not even allowed to testify as witnesses before the court against white citizens, including those accused of murder. Their "masters" could do and did whatever they wanted and the courts would not even hear a claim. Forget the Emancipation Proclamation for Blacks, this ruling lasted MUCH LONGER [until 1873] and somehow <u>went around the 13<sup>th</sup> Amendment of 1863 making emancipated slaves Americans.</u> Like the black slave horrors, this ruling effectively made white violence against Chinese Americans unprosecutable, as they had now no possibility to assert their rightful legal entitlements or claims – possibly in cases of theft or breaches of agreement – in court. The ruling remained in force until 1873. Black, White, and Yellow men were all losing the war on General Welfare and the pursuit of Liberty for their children. Just as things began to turn around President Johnson came along and started what many call the "War to Poverty". The next group is the Red people, while the actions were somewhat different; there is a limitation that should be addressed.

# Red Slavery

While many settlers left the eastern coast to find gold, and adventure, some simply had to leave. It was getting so bad in the Industrialist Northeast that many of the American inhabitants were almost forced to go west. Initially the people of the Civil War era began migrating towards the industrialist centers of our country only to find out it was not wonderful for the workers. The living conditions were unbearable, the wages were less than adequate, and the work was hard and long, mostly being accomplished by indentured and the destitute. Out of desperation, our inhabitants went a new direction to find general welfare and liberty. With all of the new weapons designed for the Civil War and the Vanderbilt railroads, this group of Americans quickly took over the area that was once owned by the American Indians. For centuries it was common practice for Indian tribes to completely annihilate one tribe and then another tribe would annihilate the victors. It was their accepted way of life. This new annihilation would come from "outsiders". As the settlers moved in, the Indians were slaughtered, moved, and ALMOST forgotten.

## Only Red People Should Kill Red People

Many people today feel that the white people had no business killing red people. Only red people were supposed to kill red people, or at least, that is what red people told them. Our schools even promoted the unfair notion that white people killed "defenseless" red people. While there is reason to believe that this was done in some cases like the case identified with Abraham Lincoln and his mass execution of the Sioux, our schools go overboard. I heard it continuously. "We should be ashamed for the actions of those slaughtering marauders", they continue to teach, "-- and if we were really ashamed, we should give the remaining Indians special privileges like not having to live by our Constitution and law, building casinos where Americans were not allowed, not paying taxes and killing eagles when it was forbidden to Americans. If those nasty white, yellow, and black people do the things that are restricted for Indians, we need to put them in prison. After all, the terrible white, yellow, and black people killed Indians over a hundred years ago and their skin color isn't right." OK! Some of the actual words are not expressed, but the crazy sentiment is there just the same.

*If any of the people who are <u>against</u> giving black skinned Americans money [Reparations] because their ancestors were slaves during and before the four Civil Wars and believe that the American Indians are somehow different and <u>should</u> get special reparations, I feel sorry for them.*

While I'm on this subject, let's think about this whole Indian reparation thing in some reasonable light. These crazy and debilitating reparations go as far as giving away huge blocks of land. Some of these blocks of land or <u>reservations</u> are larger than some of our States, all of these areas together only <u>hold a population of about 1½ %</u> of the "regular American" population, and our laws don't apply to these people in these blocks of land. Let's call them what they are- **"Indian Countries".** For those who haven't counted them, there are **588 of these countries INSIDE our borders.**

## Post War Indian Countries

From the chart below, notice that all our cities and residential areas for 98.5% of the people only add up to 4.3% of the land that makes up the United States or 98 million acres. This is about ***0.3 acres per person*** and business. The vast majority of the land is "secret land" where no living, working, residential-ing, or urbanizing is done. That is another story not covered in this book. The remaining 1.5% of the "quasi American red-people" get 56 million acres or ***12.5 acres per person*** given to them <u>rent free, tax free, and almost law free</u>. Yes, I'm talking mean about the American Indians.

| | Acres [M] | % of Total |
|---|---|---|
| Not Indian, business, or residential land | 2127 | 93.2% |
| Non-Indian Residential and Business Land. 98% of the people live work and die on this part of the United States. | 98 | 4.3% |
| Indian Reservations [1.5% of the people] | 56 | 2.5% |

The strange thing is that it isn't just one piece of land. It is hundreds of pieces. The American Government sends money to the residents. That might be OK if we got something for our money or if we were doing it for our citizens, but these people are above some of the laws that people who are not getting free land and yearly payments must abide by. Certainly, the "freedom" everyone knows is that these countries can have gambling inside their countries regardless of what the laws of the country are. Everyone has also heard about how these above the law quasi-citizens can also kill American Eagles without the normal repercussions. There are 304 different types of "reservation living groups" that are treated in this special way and given countries inside the United States Boundaries. <u>Twenty-one of the blocks of land are larger than the State of Rhode Island</u>. Several are larger than 3 or 4 of the Northeastern Statettes so sometimes we are talking about huge pieces of land. Other plots of land are small where a special group decided that they liked a different area than the large Indian countries. Remember we are talking about 588 pieces of land scattered all over the place. [That's **588 internal countries** that live outside our law, but with HUGE foreign aid].

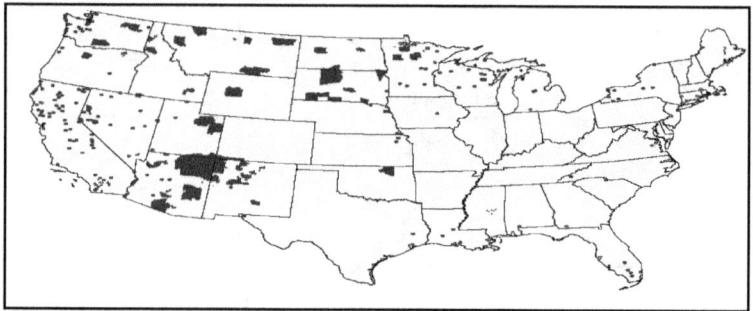

The picture above shows the **422 "country-ettes"** that are scattered around the main portion of our country and no one seems to care. Many of the land areas are worth substantial amounts of money, especially the **83 country-ettes inside the State of California**. These guys don't pay Federal, State income taxes or even sales taxes if they have business dealing inside their countries, but we pay them money every year to keep them enslaved. This is wrong.

**A Quick History**-Here's the deal. Hundreds of years ago and these guys lost a war. Rather than simply moving, they used horrible terrorist tactics to continue the insanity that are simply too horrible to discuss. If we go back a little, the Before the Europeans came; the Adena lost a war with the Ronnongwetowanca people rules most of North America until they were slaughtered by the Adena. These red people lasted until the Aztalan people annihilated them. These people ruled until the Hopewell annihilated them. On and on massacre after genocidic massacre; even if they would have had compassion on the losers, they would not have given them free land for hundreds of years and treated them as if they were better than themselves by not taxing them and still providing them money so they would not have to work.

**Burial Mounds**-In the Ohio Valley, the Adena people buried the Ronnongwetowanca under massive human filled hills as shown below. Later Indians would bury the Adena and Aztalan the same way.

**Example Battle**-In Wichita, Kansas was found the greatest prehistoric battle and burying ground yet discovered in the United States has just been found near the little town of Redlands. Here they discovered what appear to be nearly 100,000 warriors who met death in battle. With nearly 3,000 skeletons to every square acre, they were able to dig out, by the carload, hundreds of skulls and skeletons showing the signs of battle; some with as many as five arrow points sticking into it.

Maybe we should take the American Indian example and quit supporting these other countries **OR** make these guys REAL citizens of the United States. When Polish people come to America, they don't get to have their own country and neither do the Mexicans. Ok! We will get to them shortly.

---

*Either eliminate the "Indian Countries" [reservations] and don't give them continuing aid or make the Indians real citizens.*

---

Here is what we have done to the Red people. These people are probably some of the poorest quasi-Americans you can imagine simply because of these hand-outs. What we are doing is a horrible and unjust thing that goes against the Constitution. [I know there is an amendment that says we have to, but that MUST be changes ASAP.]

**Stop foreign Aid to reservation immediately**-Italy isn't still paying Etruscans for taking their land. England doesn't pay the Vikings. The Cherokee Indians don't even pay the ancient Hopewell, Azatlan, Adena, or the Ronnongwetowanca that were almost annihilated to allow for Cherokee expansion. No nation practices such absurdity. It is simply wrong and historians seem to ignore the injustice simply because the American Indians are portrayed as a victim still after hundreds of years.

> *Let's not hide behind the facts. ---Today we spend about $1.5 Billion dollars a year in foreign aid to the Indian countries under what is called the Bureau of Indian Affairs.*

Even with that, the Indians are provided assistance from other non-Indian assistance and welfare programs including those from the Oklahoma Indian Welfare Act and others. About 50% of the 1.8 million Indians in the United States live inside the Indian Reservation/countries where each family member including children are essentially given about 60 acres of land without charge. To top it off, we gave them back the right to vote outside their country without requiring them to conform to the laws of the United States.

**Rich Indians**-By the way, not all Indians are poor in fact many are extremely wealthy. If we were to classify the richest set of American Indians, it would be the Aguas Calientes of Palm Springs. While there are less than 200 individuals in this destitute tribe, the land "held by tribal trust" is worth over $1.5 Billion dollars. It seems there has been no reasonable study on the wealth of Indians to show that they, as a group, no longer need or should get our support. As long as individual Indians don't have a reasonable way of distributing wealth and many stay in abject poverty, we will continue to feel guilty.

**Sickness**-While we are on the subject of feeling guilty about Indians let me say that the red man was killed more by virulent diseases than any disruption of Indian society, or by war, or American intervention. Let me just provide you with a simple timeline of the major epidemics affecting Native Americans. Certainly, these affected all Americans, but this section is on Indians and they fared far worse than the general population.

## Bubonic Plague

- *1613-17, Bubonic Plague halved Florida's native population.*
- *1619-20, killed 60 to 80% of the New England natives [Pilgrims time]*

## Measles

- *1633-34, Measles killed up to 50% of New England and Great Lakes natives.*
- *1658-59, It struck hard again*
- *1692-93, struck again*
- *1713-15; struck New England and Great Lakes peoples*
- *1727-28; spread across the continent*
- *1768-69, struck southwestern U.S. peoples*
- *1776-78, spread from Texas to Hudson Bay*

*Each time, huge quantities of Indians met their end.*

## Malaria

- *1695-96, Malaria killed large quantities of native Americans*

## Scarlet Fever

- *1637-38, Scarlet Fever killed large quantities of New England & Great Lakes natives*

## Influenza

- *1647-48, Influenza killed large quantities of native Americans*
- *1675-76, It again killed large quantities of native Americans*
- *1761-62, It spread across North America*

## Diphtheria

- *1659-60, Diphtheria killed large quantities of native Americans*
- *1735-36, It became epidemic among New England tribes*

### Smallpox

*Smallpox is the all-time leader and still champion. This was the most devastating and wide-reaching epidemic disease to affect North America.*

- *1649-50, Smallpox killed large quantities of native Americans*
- *1639-40, then killed large quantities in New England*
- *1633-34, then killed large quantities in Great Lakes*
- *1662-63, then killed large quantities of native Americans*
- *1669-70, then killed large quantities of native Americans*
- *1687-88, then killed large quantities of native Americans*
- *1715-21, then spread at least from Texas to New England*
- *1729-30, then swept across the continent again.*
- *1738-39, then went from Texas to Hudson Bay*
- *1750-51, then went from Texas to the Great Lakes*
- *1755-56, then killed large quantities of native Americans*
- *1765-66, then killed large quantities of native Americans*
- *1779-81, then moved over all North America again*
- *1786-87; then was felt in Alaska and Canada*
- *1788-89, then came among the Pueblo Indians*
- *1815-16, then hit the Pueblo and Plains Indians*
- *1831-34, then greatly affected Plains and Great Lakes tribes*
- *1836-40, It killed native peoples of Alaska & Pueblos*
- *1843-46, then killed many Aleut to the Plains peoples*
- *1848-50, Then killed Plains and Plateau peoples*
- *1852-53, then killed Columbia River basin peoples*

- *1854-57, then killed many Plains tribes Indians*
- *1866-67, then devastated natives across the United States*
- *1876-78, It killed from St. Lawrence River to the NW Coast*
- *1897-99, then killed in tribes from California to Oklahoma.*

**Indian Losses in the South-**If we look at Civil War losses in the southern part of USA, we can probably extrapolate the devastation that diseases had on the natives. By the time of the major portion of what is known as the "Indian Wars", most of the Indians were already dead and on their way to extinction. The chart shows the losses of various Indian tribes over a period of 100 to 150 years prior to the mid-18th century. The major portions of the Indian nations had already been defeated by disease. This whole Indian guilt thing is nonsense. Non-red Americans were not the major cause of the misery and even if they contributed by unintentionally carrying germs, the whole concept seems twisted. The following chart shows the destruction of Indians by bugs. Possibly the bugs should be doing all the providing for the Indians.

| State | Tribe name | 1st date | Orig. Qty | 3rd date | now | loss |
|---|---|---|---|---|---|---|
| N.Carolina | Chowanoc | 1600 | 1500 | 1755 | 5 | 99% |
| N.Carolina | Ckeraw | 1600 | 1200 | 1768 | 50 | 96% |
| N.Carolina | Coree | 1600 | 1000 | 1707 | 50 | 95% |
| N.Carolina | Hatteras | 1600 | 1200 | 1701 | 32 | 97% |
| S.Carolina | Santee | 1600 | 1000 | 1715 | 80 | 92% |
| S.Carolina | Catawba | 1692 | 4600 | 1760 | 60 | 99% |
| S.Carolina | Cusabo | 1600 | 1200 | 1715 | 295 | 75% |
| S.Carolina | Sewee | 1600 | 800 | 1715 | 57 | 93% |
| Georgia | Guale | 1650 | 4000 | 1715 | 1215 | 70% |
| Florida | Apalachee | 1650 | 7000 | 1715 | 550 | 92% |
| Florida | Calusa | 1650 | 3000 | 1850 | 0 | 99 |
| Florida | Chatot | 1674 | 1500 | 1725 | 140 | 91% |
| Florida | Jece | 1650 | 1000 | 1728 | 52 | 95% |
| Florida | Potano | 1650 | 3000 | 1675 | 160 | 95% |
| Florida | Saturiwa | 1602 | 500 | 1675 | 30 | 94% |
| Mississippi | Houma | 1650 | 1000 | 1718 | 60 | 94% |
| Mississippi | Koroa | 1650 | 2000 | 1722 | 250 | 88% |
| Mississippi | Chakchiuma | 1650 | 1200 | 1722 | 150 | 88% |
| Mississippi | Chickasaw | 1600 | 8000 | 1715 | 1900 | 76% |
| Louisiana | Acolapissa | 1650 | 1500 | 1750 | 0 | 99% |
| Louisiana | Atakapa | 1660 | 1500 | 1850 | 0 | 99% |
| Louisiana | Bayogoula | 1650 | 1500 | 1698 | 875 | 42% |
| Louisiana | Chitimacha | 1650 | 3000 | 1784 | 54 | 98% |
| Arkansas | Quapaw | 1650 | 2500 | 1829 | 500 | 80% |

I know this section does not sound like Red Men were slaves, but they were enslaved by the very thing that is enslaving many populations in the United States today. Called Welfare, there is no welfare in it. Called subsistence, it only yanks people away from hope and pushes them into the bowels of welfare despair living only at the whim of the government. Once Indians become Americans again, we can get them out of the slave-making-poverty. This will cost less money and make our country stronger. As we consider these actions, let's look at our 2nd Declaration of Independence.

# 2nd Declaration of Independence [1776]

I think that was enough about the horrors of slavery and how slavery was the bane of our country for a long time, but let's get back to developing our 3rd Constitution that we use today. First, we need to fight a war. It would be the third President of the United Colonies, **John Hancock** [not including the Traitor Ruggles that I refuse to call President], that would be in power to sign the second Declaration of Independence we all know was established in 1776, but when was the actual 2nd Declaration made? Some have said July 4, 1776, but that is not a complete and possibly not the best answer. Here is what we know.

- **July 2, 1776-** Congress established a decree to initiate a Declaration of Independence [all but New York]
- **July 5, 1776-** This is the day President Hancock signed the Declaration giving it "clarity".
- **July 9, 1776-** This was the date New York was added to those wishing Independence.
- **August 2, 1776-** This was the date when many in Congress signed the Declaration of Independence to make it a resounding affirmation.
- **January 1777-** This was the date that the last person signed the document.
- **Never-** We never had 100% member signing as 2 Congressmen never signed. By January 1777, no one cared.

Oops, I guess July 4th isn't one of the correct dates. The document is shown next signed by our third President John Hancock.

## How did it Address Welfare and Liberty?

The document identified 3 things that would be sacred, Life, **Liberty,** and the **Pursuit of Happiness** and it changed the name of the United Colonies to the United States. It also laid claim that it is <u>their duty, to provide new Guards for their future security</u>. This is another way of saying <u>promoting the General Welfare and freedom</u> and the cost of the citizens to accomplish these things. John Hancock had signed one of the greatest declarations of all time, but just who was this guy?

## President John Hancock

To understand this great American, we have to understand sugar and molasses. The Molasses Act of 1733 was enacted by the British Parliament on the 12 colonies of America with the purpose of protecting its sugar plantations in the West Indies. This act was not designed to raise revenue but it was part of England's mercantile policy of The Molasses Act of 1733 was one of the first decisions of British Parliament that gave a real boost to John Hancock's Uncle who was smuggling in New England colonies. The Act made colonialist buy from West Indies Trading Company. High priced West Indies sugar and molasses was required for the production of RUM and Thomas Hancock exported that Rum. He needed to get molasses another way and he <u>became a great smuggler</u> bringing goods and Molasses from Jamaica, Barbados, Santo Domingo, Martinique, and colonies of Spain and France. He was so good at it that he became the wealthiest businessman in Boston. When he died, John carried on the business and people loved him for making prices lower. Tea was another of his smuggled items and when Tea Stamps threatened to restrict this enterprise, John organized the Boston Tea Party and the rest is history. I'm not saying he didn't help us become a nation, there is no question about that, but he was not altruistic in his efforts. He was a great American and an even better pirate.

After John Hancock's huge autograph on the Declaration of Independence dried, we now were officially at war and a substantial number of Presidents were elected during the war, but in 1781, we got a new Constitution called the Articles of Confederation. We need to see how this one compares concerning providing for the <u>general welfare and the pursuit of liberty for our posterity.</u>

# 2ⁿᵈ Constitution 1781

The Congress changed its name from Colonial Congress to Continental Congress to show their separation more distinctly and they adopted our second Constitution called the "Articles of Confederation". One month after the battle of Lexington, our country forefathers set up new orders, new requirements and a new President. This congressional government lasted the first 4 years of the Revolutionary War. The first President had been the first president during the 1ˢᵗ Continental Congress timing and the second President sort of was the same as the 2ⁿᵈ President during the 1ˢᵗ Congress as well. I know it's confusing, but these were confusing times. Like the 1ˢᵗ Congress, 56 delegates from 12 colonies including the sort of colony/state of Delaware convened. Georgia was still missing. Here is the gist of the 2ⁿᵈ Constitution.

## Strengths over the Previous Constitution

The Strengths of this new Constitution over the Continental Association include the following: [Some might say, today that being able to make money willy-nilly was not necessarily strength but here are commonly accepted ones.]

- *Federal Government could declare war and make peace.*
- *Federal Government could coin and borrow money*
- *Federal Government could sign treaties with foreign countries*
- *Federal Government could operate post offices*

## Weaknesses

Unfortunately, there were some weaknesses that showed up rather quickly as States began to squabble. These were fixed in the 3rd Constitution.

- *Federal Government did not have the power to tax*
- *They had no power to enforce laws*
- *Congress lacked strong and steady leadership*
- *Our government had no national Army or Navy*
- *There was no system of national courts*
- *Each State could issue its own paper money*
- *States could put tariffs on trade between states.*

## 2nd Constitution and Slavery

As noted above the condemnation of slavery was removed in the 2nd Constitution and States could allow or not allow slavery as they wished. This new Constitution was called the "Articles of Confederation". [First page is shown next]

As time went on, someone said let's rename our congress again so they did. The **"Congress of the Confederation of the United States in Congress Assembled"** lasted from 1781 to 1789. The biggest thing to note besides the war being in full swing was they were trying to get rid of the Constitution and replace it with a new one that got rid of all the free the slave stuff. Initial meetings of the 2nd Congress established a wide assortment of changes. <u>This new Constitution would finally become the governing document from March 1, 1781, until the 3rd Constitution went into effect on March 4, 1789.</u> Here is a list of the Presidents that reigned prior to this major document. There were 10 presidents that served during our 2nd Constitution. George Washington became the 1st President after our 3rd Constitution.

- **Timothy Ruggles** -<u>**First President**</u> during our <u>1st Declaration of Independence.</u> He can also be named the first Traitor President

- **Peyton Randolph** 1774- **First President** after during our <u>1st Constitution</u>

- **Henry Middleton** 1775- **First President** to become prisoner of war

- **John Hancock** 1777- **First President** when <u>our 2nd Declaration of Independence</u> was drafted and first pirate President

- **Henry Laurens** 1778- First Slave mogul President

- **John Jay** 1779 **First President** to initiate emancipation of Slaves and youngest Present EVER.

- **Samuel Huntington** 1780- First President during the 2$^{nd}$ Constitution **and possibly the first Slave President**.

## Samuel Huntington

Samuel Huntington was our 7$^{th}$ President September 28, 1779 - July 9, 1781.  He served as the last President under the 1$^{st}$ Constitution and was reelected to become the first President under the 2 Constitution. He was that good!! While there is much confusion about this man, don't tell me a poor man can't become President. According to many, this guy had been enslaved and was dirt poor during a time when not having money generally made you less than a person. I know Andrew Johnson is considered the first indentured slave President identified by most, but Samuel Huntington may also have been an indentured slave according to one of the 4 substantially different histories. If he was brought over from Scotland to work the fields of the Governor of Connecticut he would have been our first slave President rather than Andrew Johnson.  According to most histories, Samuel Huntington had no schooling, never quit learning on his own, and always pushed himself. This was the best self-made man President one could imagine. This guy was totally different that almost all Presidents in that he had a different perspective of "General Welfare and the Pursuit of Liberty for our Posterity."  Let's look at a description of this great American before he was released from slavery.

**Field Slave-**As an impoverished 'indentured servant' from Scotland, his main 'assigned task' in America had been plowing the fields of a very popular and kind Governor of Connecticut, probably Roger Wolcott. I know you are wondering why a kind man would have slaves, but this was during a time when a substantial number of people owned this type of worker and hiring a man to do field work often would result in the man leaving to find freedom in the dead of night. Slavery was a way to assure a worker stayed. Anyway, Samuel Huntington didn't want to plow his entire life and he knew some reading and writing skills from before he had been enslaved. He was able to get books from his kind master and studied all the time. Finally, unlike most, his master did not continue his enslavement and Samuel was freed and became a lawyer; a good one. He was so good; <u>he was considered one of the greatest self-made men among the founders</u> as he had mastered law without school. He was also one of the greatest legal minds of the age. Then **<u>he was elected twice as President of the United States</u>**.

## What About Andrew Johnson?

While I'm on the Slave President theme, I might as well refresh details that should have been establishing in school as there is a level of honor being the first runaway slave President. For sure Andrew Johnson's slavery was much more intense as he was a hunted runaway slave before finally becoming President of the United States. Enslaved at age 10 as an indentured "servant/apprentice" to a tailor, he, his brother William and 2 others escaped from their master in 1824 when Andrew was when 16 and his brother was 21. A reward was set for their return with a special emphasis on Andrew as detailed below.

*Notice of Runaway Apprentices*

June 24, 1824

### TEN DOLLARS REWARD.

Ran away from the Subscriber, on the night of the 15th instant, two apprentice boys, legally bound, named WILLIAM and ANDREW JOHNSON. The former is of a dark complexion, black hair, eyes, and habits. They are much of a height, about 5 feet 4 or 5 inches. The latter is very fleshy, freckled face, light hair, and fair complexion. They went off with two other apprentices advertised by Messrs. Wm. & Chas. Fowler. When they went away, they were well clad—blue cloth coats, light colored home-spun coats, and new hats, the maker's name in the crown of the hats, is Theodore Clark. I will pay the above Reward to any person who will deliver said apprentices to me in Raleigh, or I will give the above Reward for Andrew Johnson alone.

No telling what would have happened if he had been captured and sent back to his master. Instead, he hid and wandered and became the only southern Senator to stay with the Union. As Andrew was coming to Washington, Virginians captured him as set up a noose for lynching. One courageous man claimed that the people of Tennessee had requested the lynching opportunity. As Andrew was from Tennessee they let him go, temporarily. Andrew got out of there and became a running mate with Lincoln who won the presidency. Andrew got drunk. When Lincoln was killed, this previous slave decided to heal the wounds of war and established simple rules. President issued a proclamation to the defeated Agrarian States.

*If they end slavery and pledge loyalty to the USA they could send representatives to Congress.*

Everything seemed fine as the southern congressmen arrived but the other congressmen, against the law, refused to allow the new congressmen their proper place. Naturally, Johnson was as outraged as the congressmen and the citizens of the States they represented.

## Unbelievable Misdirection of the Constitution

You would think there would be something done. The sneaky Congress employed Lincoln's Secretary of War, Edwin Stanton, to begin putting burdens on the newly reentered States so Andrew Johnson fired him when he could take no more. Here is where it gets weird. Totally against the Constitution, they passed this bogus law that would not let Johnson fire any of his employees or appointments. Certainly, the Supreme Court indicated it was unconstitutional, but not before Johnson was impeached to end the first and only runaway slave President reign.

### John Jay

Sorry for the diversion, but some have not even been taught about some of these Presidents and Andrew Johnson's beginning as a runaway slave should be proclaimed, not hidden. Another important founding father is President John Jay. He was our first President to really push emancipation of slaves and he was our youngest President ever at only 34. He was younger by far than either Teddy Roosevelt [42] or John Kennedy [43] who have been acclaimed for youth. The main thing is he was the State's leading opponent of slavery. His first two attempts to pass laws for the emancipation of all slaves in New York failed in 1777, so he tried again in 1785. That failed also as New Yorkers loved having slaves. He then tried a third time in 1799 and slaves were free well after our 3<sup>rd</sup> Constitution came along. He also came up with the Manumission Society, in 1785. I know it's a stupid made up word, but it organized boycotts against newspapers and merchants in the slave trade and provided legal counsel for free blacks claimed as slaves. Besides being a judge, it seems this slavery issue was his passion.

## Presidents Under the New Constitution

The list below shows a new lot of Presidents that would try their hand at providing the <u>general welfare and pursuit of liberty.</u>

- **Thomas McKean** 1781- He was the **First President** after The British surrendered, but somehow, we forget.

- **John Hanson** 1782- He was the **First President** after war officially ended and first under a new name "United States in Congress Assembled", but somehow, we forget.

- **Elias Boudinot** 1783- He was the 10<sup>th</sup> President since the 1<sup>st</sup> Constitution.

- **Thomas Mifflin** 1784- He was the 11<sup>th</sup> and first Quaker President

- **Richard Henry Lee** 1785- Lee was our 12<sup>th</sup> President and was to draft the Declaration of Independence, but sickness had his protégé' Jefferson do it with his help.

- **John Hancock** (again) 1786- While the old smuggler was elected again, he mostly got sick and turned power over to David Ramsey who did almost everything.

- **Nathaniel Gorham** 1786- This was our First President to have to serve during our 1st Civil War [Shay's Rebellion]

- **Arthur St. Clair** 1787- This was our 15th and last President allowed to be born outside the United States [He was born in Scotland].

- **Cyrus Griffin** 1788- Griffin was our 16th President or 9th under "Articles of Confederation." He also was the last president to serve under the 2nd Constitution.

- **George Washington** 1789-1797- This is the one we remember the most. He was **1st President after the 3rd Constitution**, 10th after the 2nd Constitution, and 17th after the 1st Constitution.

As President John Hanson signed the new treaty, our country and our mind set changed. The image below shows this great change. It would be another 8 years before a third Constitution would come about.

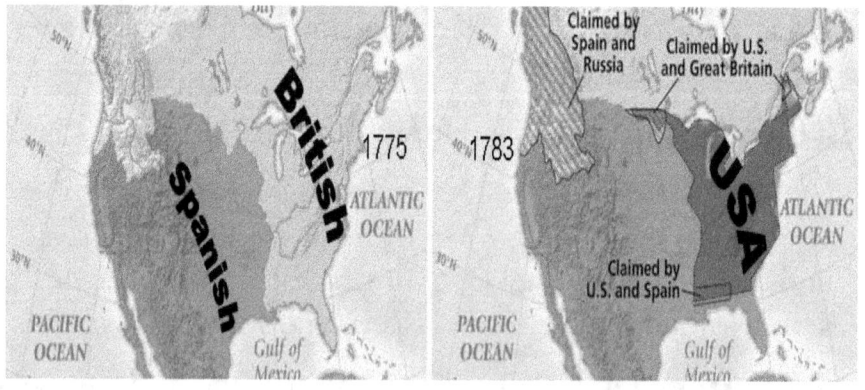

Our nation had gone through 2 Declaration of Indepenences and 3 Constitutions by the time of George Washington. Our first President is described on the following image.

# Our First President

**Timothy Ruggles**
First President After the 1st
Declaration of Independenc

**Peyton Randolph**
First President After the 1st
Constitution

**John Hancock**
First President After the 2nd
Declaration of Independence

**John Jay**
First and youngest Presiden
Pushed Freedom of Slaves

**Samuel Huntington**
First President after 2nd
Constitution[possibly slave]

**Tom Mckean**
First President after we won
the Revolution

**John Hanson**
First President after
Revolution Peace Treaty

**Nathan Gorham**
First President to encounte
a Civil War

**George Washington**
First President after the 3rd
Constitution

# Short Term Presidents

Before I get into the 3rd Constitutions, let me ask a question. What President served the shortest time? Most of the pre-3rd Constitution Presidents served for about a year, but if you said 2 hours and 4 minutes, you would have won an all-expense ---[never mind there was no prize], but I thought it would allow us to be more complete if we added the short time Presidents of the 3rd Constitution. The first one of note was in the year 1848. Zachary Taylor had won the election and would soon become the last Whig president of the United States. Unfortunately, there was a problem. He was supposed to take office on Sunday and that was against his religious convictions. The "President *pro tempore*" of the Senate at the time was Missouri senator David Rice Atchison. Therefore, he became the President for a day as Zachary had to wait until Monday. Some challenge his authority, but someone was in charge. James Polk and Vice President, George Dallas, had resigned and Taylor had refused the title. That left Atchison as our President.

**President Atchison [March 4, 1849]**

Atchison served only one day because the transfer of power was to come on a Sunday. Some say Polk even resigned his post early, on Saturday, in an effort to get back to private life as soon as possible. Whatever the reason and incident, something strange happened on March 4th and Atchison was involved. It was a glorious day for President Atchison and very few scandals occurred during his presidency. One scandal might be notable and we should bring it up. President Atchison evidently <u>slept through almost his entire "term in office"</u>. This was done either out of fatigue or because of the after-effects of the Saturday night inaugural parties. Now "that" is the profile of a true leader.

## Not the Shortest Reign as President

While only being President for 24 hours is short, his reign was by no means the shortest. Three times, the Vice Presidents have had to assume the power of the Presidency.

- **President G.H.W. Bush's first Assignment**-Ronald Reagan had to undergo surgery on July 13th, 1985 for cancerous polyps near his colon. He wrote a letter to both the Speaker of the House and the President pro tempore, announcing his incapacity. Therefore, George H.W. Bush acted as President from 11:28 AM to 7:22 PM, when Reagan sent another letter, announcing he was once again capable of serving as president.
- **President Dick Cheney**-The same situation occurred when George W. Bush underwent colonoscopy in 2002. Vice-President Dick Cheney acted as president for several hours. [June 29, 2002- 2 hour and 15 minutes]
- **President Dick Cheney's Second Term**- In 2007 G.W Bush became ill again and Vice President Cheney

became our president for a few hours again. [July 20, 2007 -2 hours and 4 minutes]

Adding the service of all three of these short-timers together was less than President Atchison's presidency so don't even think about ignoring his term.  By the way, isn't it strange that all three of these last Presidential assignments were caused by the colon?  With that let's go to the third Constitution of the United States.

# 3rd Constitution 1789

Finally, we get to the one everyone remembers. Some call it the Pro-Slavery Constitution. While the first 2 Constitutions eliminated or seemed to restricted Slavery, the one ratified during Cyrus Griffin's Presidential term in office not only seemed to encourage it, it placed specific characterizations about slaves not being "Real People". Here is an excerpt.

## Article I

*"Representatives and direct taxes shall be appointed among the several States which may be included within this union, according to their respective numbers, which shall be determined by adding to the whole number of free persons* **[again indicating that non-free people were unacceptable or they would not provide the distinction]**, *including those bound to service for a term of years, and excluding Indians, not taxed, **three fifths of all persons**.'* Therefore, slaves were not even considered a whole person in a census. A slave was only 3/5th of a person.

## Article IV

*No person held in service or labor in one State, under the laws thereof, escaping to another, shall, in consequence of any law or regulation therein, be discharged from such service or labor, but shall be delivered up on claim of the party to whom such service or labor may be due.*

That's a long drawn out way of saying that if you find a slave; you must return him to his owner. After all they are only 3/5ths of a person. Make no mistake, it is not talking about prisoners held by a State it is talking about prisoners held by individuals. The direct indication that "ANY PARTY" could claim the "laborer held in servitude" allows an individual to own a person.

*We the People of the United States, in Order to form a more perfect Union, establish Justice, insure domestic Tranquility, provide for the common defense, promote the General Welfare, and secure the Blessings of Liberty to ourselves and our Posterity, do ordain and establish this Constitution for the United States of America.*

**Form a More Perfect Union-**This means that the rights of each person and each State would be made equal or as equal as possible and for religions not being hampered by the government as we learn later.

**Establish Justice-**This means the rights defined by a majority would be assured for all. While this did not include Indians or Slaves, there were provisions later to involve them as well.

**Insure Domestic Tranquility-**Elimination of Fear and strife.

**Provide the Common Defense-**Protection of our country controlled by a federally mandated Army and Navy. The following image shows the beginning of this great document that is so often misquote, abused, and trampled.

## General Welfare and Secure Liberty

This last part of the preamble is the main part that has been sorely misquoted and abused. Welfare payments that are taxed if someone works are the exact opposite to welfare of a population like our United States. When the framers added the blessings of liberty it eliminated the giving of money without work. The idea we call those types of payments welfare is totally different than this passage is trying to establish. Instead to establishing liberty and GENERAL welfare, the payments tear down the very fiber of a democracy and our republic. There is no question those payments disrupt and tear down the general welfare of our country as we will see and they completely destroy the opportunity to secure the blessings of liberty. Liberty is a funny word. On one hand liberty is the opposite of promoting welfare, but on the other hand they go hand in hand. Many times, the second half of the welfare statement is used for newspapers being allowed to print what they work for but there is more to that part of the preamble as well.

I know this sounds like some hard-hearted analysis driven by greed but it is not. We need to protect our poor and we need to protect all Americans. Sometimes we need to protect them from themselves. If you ever wondered why socialist and communist governments fail, it is the "joy of freedom part". In a communist government, people are pushed into a desperate need for the government to take care of them so all freedom is lost.

*Freedom REQUIRES independence or independence REQUIRES work to allow for freedom.*

A government that does not establish a limit on loss of independence will certainly fail and general welfare will be lost. It appears we are losing our welfare and freedom with earned income credit, food stamps, free housing, free medical and all the rest. Luckily, there is a way back to reason.

# Don't Forget the Word General

The main thing to notice is this particular "welfare" is not an individual mandate but a **GENERAL** mandate securing the welfare of <u>our nation as a whole</u>. When the statement continues it say provide for the pursuit of Liberty for **OUR** posterity.

*One might suggest on one level this could simply say Americans should be assured jobs and <u>elimination of fear that their livelihood will be taken away by government intervention.</u>*

I would talk about the elimination of coal mining in America here, but I want to provide this data in a more organized fashion. I would talk about allowing farm consortiums to bring in foreign workers while Americans lose a work opportunity. I might even bring up the statistics that says a part time employed woman with 2 children making $29,000 has a higher standard of living that a full-time employed woman making 69 thousand dollars, but I think I'll wait on that and not bring it up. Sorry, but I just have to say that it would be stupid for the part time employee should ever attempt advancement as it would be almost impossible. Fear possibly sets in as her dependence turns her world into a communistic nightmare. Even if she doubled here apparent salary, she would have substantially less. We can say the same for the $69,000 dollar a year woman as she is missing out on her children more and possibly even has a sore back and the only reward is the JOY of FREEDOM.

## Freedom

Unlike the ideals of the Communist and Socialist Manifestos this Constitution was dedicated to freedom, with freedom there is an awful price to pay.

*Those who work-eat. Those who don't work and can don't eat. The "and can" part is only added in a Republic rather than a Democracy. In a free society, even those not able to work would starve, but there must be limits on freedom to secure domestic tranquility so we will investigate that element.*

Freedom is a harsh sentiment. Many American's gambled their comforts in the pursuit of freedom and found unmeasurable hardships, but they were free. Most lived, but some died for their freedom, not by an outside enemy and not by communistic rot taking away their soul, but because of freedom.

*Could this Nastiness be What the Constitution says?*

The simple answer to that is characterized in what John F Kennedy stated.

*It is not what your country can do for you; **it is what you can do for your country.***

He proclaimed, there <u>are no free tickets</u> here, just security that hard work will not be ignored. Some like this form of government and some like Communism---at least until everyone is so destitute that hunger is common, long lines to find meager items in limited shopping centers, and no one is allowed to worship his God. It is a slow agonizing death.

As soon as Kennedy died, the acting President Johnson quickly got rid of all semblance of Kennedy's statement. He rolled out what would be one of the <u>most devastating attempts at destroying the General Welfare</u> every thought about. Called a "War of Poverty", everyone knew it would be a ***war towards poverty***, but few resisted. I will show the data about what his disregard of the Constitution actually has done to most citizens of our once great country. Before we get into today's issues and constitutional breaches that are taking are our freedom and enslaving our population let's first reach back to the time when our country was almost lost over 150 years ago. The time was the 1860s and 1870s. Instead of destruction by having everyone on government supplied welfare payments, our country was ransacked by uncontrolled big business. Instead of becoming communistic, our country felt the evils of Fascism.

*Given limitless natural resources, an unfettered democracy will always be pushed into Fascism where industries take control of the country.*

Fascism always feels great at the beginning as industries flourish and terms like Industrial Revolution is heard as the industries take over the country and massive Industrialist clubs form to expand their profits and control and the distance between the poor and the wealthy spiral out of control. During this time our Constitution was disregarded and multiple billionaires-controlled Congress, the Presidency, and the country.

# Spread of Disunity

If we want to look at a beginning of this horrible downfall, there are many dates that could be used. I am only using the 1860s because the abuses were so hidden that most have no recollection of them and our nation was almost destroyed. While the 4th Civil War that occurred at this time didn't help, I'm talking about the destruction by government sponsored, government funded, industrialization of monopolize commodities. The commodities were under-control for a time, but then Railroadians, Steel Manufacturers, Land speculators, Gold manipulators and others. If you went against the 'Controlled" Presidents of this time, you could find yourself in a hidden prison. The first was named Abraham Lincoln, but Ulysses Grant was just as bad. As the war began, a large number of influential people rejected what the people knew to be the President's War. Those who voiced their apprehension disappeared.

### Lincoln Mysterious Prisons

Rather than discussion these things, here is an excerpt from a New York Magazine that saw Lincoln's reign first hand. He was accused of having little or no trial and isolated confinement for large numbers of people who were against him.

**"The Old Guard / Volume 1, Issue 5, May 1863"**- *The author of this work was for <u>several months confined in one of Mr. **Lincoln's** bastilles, and was finally let out, as hundreds of others have been, without a trial, and without</u>*

*being informed of the reason of his incarceration. In this book, Mr. Mahony has paid the Administration back with interest, for its criminal assaults upon his liberty. He has tried to kill the country. Instead of sewing him in a leather sack, with a cock, a viper, and an ape, we have allowed him to literally overwhelm us with an army of his official vermin. His cocks and vipers, and apes, swarm upon us like a cloud of locusts.*

## Lincoln's Slave Buying Idea

Having and working well over a million slaves, Lincoln was having issues with Kentucky, West Virginia, Missouri, Tennessee, Delaware, and Maryland. They continued to have no idea that his Civil War had somehow turned into a war to eliminate slaves. They simply thought the south had revolted from the 49% taxes imposed on them to force their purchase of high priced Northern materials provided by Lincoln's Industrialist friends. Lincoln came up with a plan to buy the slaves so the nation would not falter any more than he had already yanked it apart. He decided that he would purchase slaves at $400 per head and give another $100 per head to get rid of the black people by transporting them to either Liberia or Haiti. It seemed like a good plan to him.

**Buying Started**- On April 10, 1862, Congress declared that the Federal government would compensate slave owners who freed their slaves to be exported. Slaves in the District of Columbia were freed on April 16, 1862 and their owners were duly compensated. The cost was estimated to have been about a million dollars to free 3000 slaves. It is believed the million dollars was used by the recipients to purchase "Indentured Servants", but that is another story.

**Backfire**-The confused slaveholding UNION States which could not believe that the war had something to do with the elimination of slavery in the United States. Lincoln wanted to purchase slaves from all northern slave owners which would have been over $100,000,000 to appease the northern slaveholders but most of the <u>northern</u> Slave States could not believe that the United States would outlaw the owning of slaves. Congress signed a "second" 13$^{th}$ Amendment only month after purchasing thousands of slaves and getting letters of concern from the other slave States that had stayed with the Union. All Slaves were free and the remaining States got no compensation.

*Little did the UNION slave States know that the Congress would operate without ANY of the Slave-State representation. Certainly, it was against the Constitution desire for the <u>General Welfare</u> of Americans from all States and the pursuit of liberty, but who cares about law when you can make it up as you go along.*

Kentucky, Virginia, Missouri, Tennessee, Delaware, and Maryland in the Union States all balked at the absurd notion that slaves should be freed. That was not what they signed up for during the 4$^{th}$ Civil War. Here is an excerpt of their horror. [This text below is talking about the huge money spent to help Lincoln constituent, slave owners in Maryland and what he would owe them.]

*At the same rate of valuation [of slaves to be bought by taxes], these would amount to $358,833,600 <u>Add for deportation and colonization, $100 each</u> $119,244,533 and we have the enormous sum of $478,078,133. We did not feel that we should be justified in voting for a measure, which, if* *carried out, would add this vast amount to our public debt,* *----The right to hold slaves is a right appertaining to all the States of this Union. They have the right to cherish or abolish the institution as their tastes or their interests may prompt, and no one is authorized to question the right, or limit its enjoyment. And no one has more clearly affirmed that right than you have.* -- *It is enough for our purpose to know that it is a right; and so, knowing, we did not see why we should now be expected to yield it."*

*No one EVER believed the war had to do with Slavery. That was **MADE UP** much later.*

**Statette Control of the Union-** The tiny New England Statettes were generally the only group pushing the fast elimination of black slavery rather than the slow reductions already in place. With no Southern Congressmen the New Englanders were in substantial control of this illegal Congress. They ran all the committees and the insured that States being brought in would have less per-capita voting rights by making all new States slightly larger than Rhode Island. Texas, for instance is a little larger than Rhode Island, Connecticut, Vermont, New Hampshire, Delaware, Massachusetts or New Jersey. Here is another article from the Union Magazine "The Old Guard". This is what New Yorkers had to say.

*"To Realize how completely the New England school of politicians has seized the Government of the United States, we have only to refer to the following list of the chairmen of all the important committees of the Senate:*

| Committee. | Chairman | Where from. |
|---|---|---|
| Foreign Relations. | Sumner. | New England. |
| Finance. | Fessened | New England. |
| Military Affairs | Wilson. | New England. |
| Naval Affairs. | Hale. | New England. |
| Post Offices. | Collemar. | New England. |
| Pensions. | Foster. | New England. |
| Claims. | Clark. | New England. |
| Public Buildings. | Foote. | New England. |
| Contingent Expenses. | Dixon. | New England. |

*Practically, the United States Senate might just about as well meet in Boston as in Washington. The same preponderance of Yankee abolitionism is found in the committees of the Lower House. The fifteen millions of people in the Middle and Western States are used as a tail to the New England abolition kite. These shapers of New England thus control over $800,000,000 per annum of the money of the country. The great States of New York, Pennsylvania, and of the West, have comparatively no voice in the management of the finance of the country. Its monetary and political destiny is in the hands of a set of crazy fanatics. If a country thus used and thus abused can survive, either financially or politically, it will be a miracle indeed.*

*So here is what we have-- 11 States with no representation, 17 States with limited representation and 7 tiny New England Statettes that together were smaller than the single State of Virginia running the country.*

With that little bit of Constitutional abuse, let's discuss the thing called Emancipation Proclamation that in no way established emancipation.

# "Not" Emancipation Proclamation

The main theme of the proclamation had nothing to do with ending Slavery It had to do with eliminating Constitutional law. It proclaimed **"punishment to those who were part of the insurrection"**, not "freedom for slaves". People were angry at the pictures of battles and they wanted the "Rebels" to pay.

*If you remember, 10 percent of the slaves were owned by people on Lincoln's side of the war.*

Therefore, old Lincoln had to come up with something different than simply freeing slaves or he would become and even less popular President and that is not a good thing for a President. Let me first state the more correct truth below and then I will provide the details afterwards.

### Abraham Lincoln

He was noted for freeing the slaves with the Emancipation Proclamation, but it did not. Don't get me wrong. He still was a pretty good President in spite of himself and worked to free slaves "after" the proclamation, but not because of it. The southern States were not against him because they feared losing slavery. All they knew was that he was destroying their States by establishing terrible tariff laws and most of the United States knew this fact. There was no question in the minds of most people of the time, including

Lincoln, but somehow, things have been twisted out of proportion to cover up the huge Constitutional violations all through this time.

## Insurrection Punishment Proclamation

As I mentioned above, many of the so-called slave States did not rebel with the other agrarian States so Lincoln didn't free the slaves of any State that was part of the United States with his Emancipation Proclamation. Instead, he used "slave elimination" as punishment for "**rebels only**", if and when those States were forced to become part of the United States again. He also reprimanded and replaced his generals who overstepped their calling by freeing slaves indiscriminately along the Border States.

## Lincoln Made It Clear

In his punishment statement, Lincoln clearly indicated that **only** the States in rebellion would lose the ability to have slaves. All the other slave owners could beat, kill, trade, rape, and abuse their slaves without interference. Let's read the portion of the proclamation that is continually misinterpreted. This section of the proclamation was entitled "An Act to Suppress Insurrection, to **Punish** Treason and Rebellion" and it was approved by the Congress [run by New England] on July 17, 1862. I mentioned it earlier, but it is worth repeating. I highlighted the important parts. [Just like the name of the document which is completely different than "Let's free the slaves", the whole speech had nothing to do with ending slavery.] Anyway!!! Here is the section most misinterpreted by casual readers and by teachers of our children.

# Act to Suppress Insurrection, to Punish Treason & Rebellion

*"And be it further enacted, that all slaves of persons who shall* **hereafter** *be engaged in rebellion against the government of the United States, or who shall in any way give aid or comfort thereto, escaping from such persons and taking refuge within the lines of the army; and all* **slaves captured from such persons** *or deserted by them and coming under the control of the government of the United States; and all slaves of such persons found or being within any place occupied by rebel forces and afterwards occupied by the forces of the United States, shall be deemed* **captives of war**, *and* **shall be forever free** *of their servitude, and not again held as slaves."* Let's repeat what it says just in case some teacher is still out there expounding on the misinterpreted idea that this proclamation freed the slaves:

*Only slaves that were taken as "captives of war" would be freed. All others must remain slaves; especially the 350 thousand plus individuals under slavery in the States that didn't leave the union. It was like saying he would free all slaves that were not in the United States of America.*

I think one technicality should be determined here as well. The document was only for States or citizens that would engage in rebellion After the July 17, 1862 date. To my knowledge, no additional States rebelled after that time so it was a misworded edict in the first place.

## Lincoln Promoted Slavery

Just to reinforce this weirdness, let's examine the following edit by Lincoln and resolve its implications. I call that his

"Keep Slavery Speech" which was proclaimed to CLARIFY the first thing.

*"And be it further enacted, That no slave escaping into any State, Territory, or the District of Columbia, from any other State, shall be delivered up, or in any way impeded or hindered of his liberty, except for crime, or some offence against the laws, <u>unless the person claiming said fugitive shall first make oath that the person to whom the labor or service of such fugitive is alleged to be due is his lawful owner,</u> and has not borne arms against the United States in the present rebellion, nor in any way given aid and comfort thereto; ..."*

*Wow! The Emancipation Proclamation would free slaves unless the owner said he owned them.* ***Now that is what I call emancipation.***

What a great speech to be remembered for! Another thing Lincoln should be remembered for is slave buying.

### Lincoln Bought Slaves

As I mentioned before Lincoln decided to be one of the biggest Slave purchasers of the United States. Each one he bought he would get money from the Congress to ship them out of the country. What a mess. I'm not going over it again, but he was having a difficult time getting rid of the newly freed slaves. Here is his new proclamation.

### Lincoln's Slave Purchase Deal

*"And the executive will, in due time, recommend that all citizens of the United States who shall have remained loyal thereto throughout the rebellion, shall (upon the restoration of the constitutional relation between the United States, and*

*their respective States, and people, if that relation shall have been suspended or disturbed) be* __compensated for all losses by acts of the United States, including the loss of slaves.__ *"*

## New York Magazine Speaks Again

Here is what "The Old Guard" had to say in its January 1863 edition.

*"The Lower House of Congress has passed a bill to appropriate ten million dollars of the people's money to buy the negroes in Missouri.—Congress has no power to appropriate the people's money for such an object—no more right to empty the treasury of the United States to buy negroes in Missouri, than it has to buy negroes in Guinea—or, than it has to pass a law authorizing Mr. Lincoln to send out his provost marshals to rob the pockets, and steal the shirts from the backs, of every man they can overtake. The administration has been for some time spending more than one hundred thousand dollars a day, to support negroes whom they have stolen, or induced to run away from their masters. And all this outlay for negroes has been going on while our soldiers have remained unpaid, and their wives and children are suffering with want—almost with starvation Within the last thirty days, over one hundred thousand white men— North and South—have been slain to appease the terrible Moloch -- It is the death-warrant of the nation. Born to impoverish and destroy white men, to bestow an imaginary and unattainable good upon black men. Will the people pay the unlawful debt? For one, I am resolved not to go into this negro-buying business if I can help it. If the people of Missouri wish to get rid of their negroes,*

95

*they are welcome—provided they do not throw them upon us for support. If they do not wish to get rid of them, they are welcome to keep them. Only the people of these Northern States are determined that they will not be taxed to buy them. Let those who wish invest in that kind of fund; only let them understand that they have Mr. Lincoln and his crazy Congress for paymasters. I, Abraham Lincoln & Co., promise to pay ten millions of dollars for the aforesaid negroes of Missouri. If anybody is content with such a note of hand they can take it; but let them not imagine that the nation will ever endorse it. If capitalists are content to advance money on such paper, it is their own speculation; let them not accuse the nation of dishonesty in repudiating the illegal demand.*

*You guessed it, the New England run Congress gave money to buy black slaves and ship them to Africa and Central America.*

### Quick! Let's Change the Law

It would seem that just about everyone [in New England] loved the "I want to buy slaves" tax initiated by the President, so what other skullduggeries were up Mr. Lincoln's sleeves. Almost immediately, after the remaining slaves were bought by the United States, Congress passed the [NEW] 13th amendment [1865]. Let's read a small portion and see how sneaky they were. This should be called the "Since We Bought the Slaves Already, We Can't Buy Slaves" Amendment.

### The Second Thirteenth Amendment

*"Neither the United States nor any State shall assume or pay any debt or --any claim for the loss or emancipation of*

*any slave; but all such debts, obligations and claims shall be held illegal and void."*

Sound fishy to me. Only after they have accomplished the buying of slaves from the select few, did they claim that the deed of paying for slaves was evil.

---

*The whole congress should have gone to prison over this one. How dare they pass such a law after just being the major violators.*

---

## The Illegal Proclamation

Not only did the Emancipation Proclamation only address punishment of the Rebel States by taking their slaves, without compensation, it was completely against the law outlined in the Constitution of the United States. Let's read article 4 of the Constitution.

---

*According to Article 4, if a slave is found outside his State, he must be returned to his owner and cannot be kept in the other State as a safe haven. [I paraphrased it, but you can read it yourself any time you want.]*

---

Not only does the article above eliminate the possibility of doing what the president did, but also the Constitution clearly States the following:

---

*ALL rights not expressly given to the federal government were in ALL cases to be considered States Rights.*

---

## Illegal Proclamation

The Emancipation Proclamation illegally took some slaves away as a punishment and allowed others. The subsequent changes to remove State control from almost all areas of our government have all been in violation of the Constitution. NONE of it is written in our history books.

Here again I must emphasis that just because the emancipation document was illegal--

*It doesn't mean that elimination of slavery was wrong. Of course, it was right. Just the method was wrong.*

Also, the more recent changes making our federal government more powerful than allowed by the Constitution may or may not be a good thing. The point here is that these "changes" and "illegal actions" should be taught to our children along with all the comfortable stuff so that they can have a small chance at reaching the truth.

# Against the Law Amendments

The Constitution had held strong for 61 years, but due to the fact that the Southern States were without Representation during the reconstruction period, the Constitution was changed, and changed, and changed again. After 1871, it would not be changed again for another 43 years. All laws and amendments to the Constitution passed during this time were clearly not the desire of representatives of Americans, but instead were the desires of a small group of Industrialist Americans "only" voted in by a tiny group of Senators from the New England Statettes. They should rightfully be removed and reintroduced so that all States could vote on the illegal Amendments. **The three Amendments in question [13th through the 15th] are described below.**

I don't mean that the 11 rebel States didn't have "representatives" voting, I mean it was worse than not voting. If they had not voted, then, at least, the will of the non-rebellious Americans would have been known. The "Mock representatives of the rebel States" were shipped in by unscrupulous Industrialists to absolutely insure that almost ALL Americans would lose their level of representation except for those who paid for the "mock representatives".  For those not told of the treachery, the lower States were illegally carved into 5 military controlled States under a law called the Military Reconstruction Act (until a new Constitution could be drawn up). Of course, the law was against the Constitution and placed into use by the even more powerful New Englanders, but that isn't the worst. These generals selected those who would be congressmen from the South. Unbelievably, the fake senators and Congressmen voted to continue the horrors of governing without a Constitution for 5 years AFTER the war ended. While the fake congress was doing all types of things to under-mind the structure and freedom of the United States, they sent up a smoke screen in the form of the 13th, 14th, and 15th Amendments. We will look at these horrible pieces of legislative criminality issued with half of the country's representation missing.

# The Unstable Democracy

## United States Fascism

If a government strongly looks after the rights of the extremely rich Industries owned by a tiny group of extremely people over those of the majority of the citizens, then the society is Fascist. [During the mid to end of the 19th century, a dozen of the wealthiest industrialists controlled the legislative branch of our government. The top 0.01 percent of Americans controlled almost 50 percent of all of the money that was being established.]

*Here is a rule of thumb - The wealthiest 0.01% should not control over 20% of the money or the DEMOCRACY is gone. Another way to say it is that the average wealth of the top 0.01% should not be more than 100 times that of the average person. In a 300-million-person society, that is the top 30 thousand. In the 1870s with a population of only 38 million that was the top 4 thousand.*

## Socialism

The government can go to the other extreme very quickly. If the government strongly looks after the rights of the poor, lazy, under-achieving, or undeserving in violation of the rights of the majority, then the might of the government to control such actions becomes too strong to control. This also stifles business and growth except for business providing protection to the government entity [the military]. This type of society is typically called Socialist. This is started when many poor families are given money not to work. If they try to work, the government typically punishes them by taking away some of their "free" money. The poor families are given more money if they have children and still more if they remain unmarried. Medical needs are typically paid for if an individual is poor, but when they decide to go back to work, the government takes away the medical opportunities. All these things give power to the government and are symptoms of its eventual takeover and complete slavery to the government.

## Welfare

The power is exemplified by government placing strict payment requirements on industry, the entrepreneurial rich and the middle class. This burden quickly reduces productivity and increases the wealth of those inside the government. The loss of productivity hurts the middle class even more than the fascist society. Eventual doom of the society occurs until a strong dictator backed by the military machine arises to force the poor back to work. As can be derived from the above, this type of event is worse than the Fascist society so we need to guard against this one as well.

*Here is another rule of thumb - The government entity should control less than 25% of the country's wealth or the DEMOCRACY or Republic is in jeopardy.*

## Overview of the Overview

While the above descriptions are way too generalized to be useful, they show that democracy is a fleeting thing ready to be whisked away at a moment's notice. In almost all instances of government control, the super-rich and super poor are targets for special treatment in today's societies so modern societies have both special interest groups controlling portions of the government. We need a new name. A democracy or Republic cannot stand with only the Fascist interests nor can it survive with only Socialist desires. <u>It MUST have 2 strong antagonistic parties to survive.</u>

*A more reasonable term for the modern Republic should be Fascist Socialism.*

## A Time Without Fascist Socialism

Without the 2 very strong antagonistic parties, the country will INEVITABLY convert to the methodology of the much stronger group. For a time, the United States had only one party, the Republican Party. From 1860 until 1884, there was no antagonist and the Republic was lost. Let me call this period the "socialistically hidden fascist years". [Sorry for the Civics overview. I'll get back on track below.]

# Controlled Republic

Fascism is controlled by strict limits on monopoly, business practice, unionization of the workforce, and regulation. So long as there is reason in this style of government things begin to settle out with some restriction in expansion to allow for the General Welfare and pursuit of liberty. The Sherman Anti-trust Act began the Republic-ation of our nation. Monopolies were split up for a time, and intermediate wars helps regulate our country's fixation with self- interest was replaced by a level of patriotism that flowed everywhere. Growth was reestablished, our position as a world power expanded, businesses increased their international base and the strength of our country became well known as the standard of living of Americans during the 1940s and 1950s rose and fell periodically, but always to allow for a new level of pride in country. Soon is would all go away as a new term began to push into our country and into the political arena. The words were sweet; Free love, free expression, protecting the poor, expanding the rights of employees, security for the poor. All was a smokescreen to communism.

# Can We have Communism and Freedom?

Some claim we can have both. We can allow those who don't work to meet a limited level of existence simply because it is the right thing to do, not thinking about the nation as a whole. Most of these people have gone out to see if there is work, but found none so they did their part. Today over 50% of the Americans are compensated for not working in some way. Many of those make their entire livelihood by government handouts. Some have to claim that the downward spiral of government handout living has been going on for generations in a family. With half the population voting to either get governmental money or starving with no job opportunity, the cycle is assured to continue until the end of a society. First will be the transition into a formal communist government which is followed by vast levels of poverty or a trumped-up monetary system until it all falls apart. Greece is beginning to see the end. Rome died that way and most other societies lost their freedom slowly. Some of those holding to the rich rewards of passive hand-outliving believe they will be dead before the end comes so there is no downside. The problem is we had children.

### Limits of General Welfare

We are going to try to understand the limits of General Welfare, what it means, how it can be enacted and how we can begin change the mindset and start to be responsible, patriotic, citizens doing "for our country". Some say it is simply too late, but there is a seed of freedom in Americans that cannot be broken. We can develop the seed and spring a new unified country if we take the hard steps.

## Steps to Freedom

Here are some of the steps needed. You won't like them all and you may even fell sick to your stomach with some, but our country is festering, and spiraling into a death which will be far worst to all. The answer to the original question is we cannot have communism and Freedom. Simply calling it socialism doesn't help either.

- *We Must Control Workforce Expansion*
- *We Must Establish Jobs, not Slavery*
- *We Must Eliminate Glamorized Poverty*
- *We Must Slow the Welfare Spiral*
- *We Must Reduce the Stronghold of Monopolies*
- *We Must Limit Punishments to Offset Republic Ideals*
- *We Must Establish More Control over Greed*
- *We must teach our children about how to work for liberty, not freedom from work driving them to slavery*
- *We must not punish the majority by coddling deviates, militants, and the godless*
- *We must support marriage, not punish it*
- *We must bring pride in America back by focusing on helping the majority rather than killing the middle class.*

By doing these steps, our country has a chance. Without doing something different, we are doomed no matter how well someone wrote a Constitution.

# Control Workforce Expansion

A country is built on resources. In America, vast amounts of natural resources are coupled with the ingenuity and drive associated with something we can call the <u>blessings of Liberty we give to ourselves and our posterity.</u> We saw this special something during World War II especially as our country united and we became the absolute masters of the world for a time. In a different way, the same resource of liberty minded colonists was responsible for some of the outcome that would initially build our Country. I know a lot of the victory stemmed from the short-sided vision of the British, but for many, the beginnings of our nation was a do or die consideration brought on by a national fervor and pride. Both of these factors, natural resources and the lust for liberty, work together, only when growth of both are combined and in unison. If natural resources are too quickly diminished, the country is lost. If the population loses its patriotic population and desire for freedom, the country is lost. One of the most devastating ways to lose patriotic populations is by elimination of jobs. Our founders and subsequent lawmakers established a reasonable way to reduce the devastation of loss of jobs. This was by restriction in population growth. As the nation expanded, entry of immigrants allowed for expansion of jobs. As the growth subsided, restrict was not only desirable, it was of immeasurable need. We could not take away the livelihood of Americans and survive. Today, everything is all out of control. We must remove the huge numbers of illegal aliens in our country. I know some have told you these people were immigrants, but that simply is not so. A country has a specific limit to resources including jobs, land, civilization, structures for commerce, food, etc. and <u>we must regulate how fast or slow our country expands</u> so that the opportunity for freedoms exist in our country. It has been successfully accomplished 2 times in the 20<sup>th</sup> century and if it is not done again, we will soon lose our rightful place in the world. We will soon lose the capability to provide for the General Welfare. We will soon be in a death spiral.

## Promote the General Welfare

Just what does it mean to promote the General Welfare anyway? Our federal Government does some of this. Certainly, there is general protection of the land and assurance of some reasonable existence, but the ones that have been in the news lately are in three parts; protection of our livelihood, protection from internal and external enemies, and protection from greed. There are many issues that are touched by this one term, but one that is most misunderstood is the capture and deportation of harmful illegal aliens that I previously mentioned. Only a couple of brave Presidents in the last 80 years have done their duty to the Constitution and to America in this regard. I know deportation sounds heartless and cruel to those outside the United States, but let me tell you something important. If the President and Congress keep doing nothing about this elimination of jobs, artificial reduction of wages, putting substantial pressures on monetary capabilities of our government, and the unsupportable care of those who are not Americans, our own country will die.

---

*Have you ever heard the ridiculous notion that if we removed illegal aliens in an effort to assure the common welfare of the Americans by reducing pressure on our job market jobs, reducing infiltration of those owing allegiance and patriotism to other countries, and limiting entrance of those who would instigate harm on Americans, would backfire?*

---

- Some have said there is no harm in flooding our country with people without control as our joblessness and cost to support those entering skyrockets. I know you think these "migrants" are taking nasty jobs and helping our country, but <u>this is all a lie</u> as billions and billions are being provided to keep these people alive.

- Some have said there can be no issue with allowing uncontrolled millions aligned with countries outside our borders as they are just as patriotic as the next American, but <u>that is a lie</u> as American honored events are being forgotten and replaced by those that do not offend outsiders.

- Some have said Americans have too much and should allow those with less to infiltrate our borders at the cost of hardship to Americans because it makes those who don't lose their livelihoods feel better. <u>This is a lie</u>. There are no winners in this practice, not even the intruders.

- Many have said getting rid of these criminals from our workforce would be a failure as no one would take the menial jobs and America would suffer severely!! <u>This is a lie.</u> Once the anti-Constitution payments are reduced, people will work and begin winning back their freedom. Certainly, you cannot make getting a job a punishment as the system is today.

I want you to think about this just a little as we find millions of high school and college kids unable to find work. Think about it as our reducing standard of living and welfare rolls are such that <u>over half of Americans</u> now are getting money and aid from our government [to survive] rather than having the resources to support it as John Kennedy told Americans was their duty. Think about it as America's Day was recently banned from a High School so that it would not "offend anyone". Think about it as wages are artificially driven downward as illegal workers stay quiet when their "Owners" pay them much less than Americans eliminating opportunity of Americans having those same jobs and the gestapo control of the farming industries and other task masters are loosed.

### Hoover Successfully Tested

Twice in the recent history of the United States the welfare of our population was put ahead of politics by limiting and reducing the illegal inrush of foreigners taking jobs away from our citizens and overburdening our relief programs which assured less money for job establishment programs. The two courageous Presidents were **Herbert Hoover** and **Dwight Eisenhower**. Herbert Hoover was faced with huge increases in illegal entrance into the US because of the efforts of the huge farm consortiums and the power of the Senate, but by 1931 Hoover greatly reduced the massive influx of aliens in 1931 by one simple act. Under the careless arms of Roosevelt, the influx began increasing by leaps about bounds finally reaching an increase of 6000%. As Hoover came to power there was no reductions, but Eisenhower, in 1953, found a way to deport and encourage the leaving of as many as 3 million illegals. Possibly both actions were career limiting, but their fortitude to protect Americans and our Constitution may have saved us for a time.

# Herbert Hoover [1931]

Herbert Hoover's actions assured <u>over a million illegal aliens were deported and tens of thousands work visa aliens "encouraged" to leave</u>. This operation would be known as "Operation Wetback" just like later operations but this one was in 1931. This President took what would today be considered a politically unpopular position by rounding up and deporting illegal aliens to create jobs for US Citizens. This first attempt occurred shortly after the banker-induced Stock Market Crash of 1929 when President Herbert Hoover ordered the round-up and deportation of illegals by the US Immigration and Naturalization Service. The Hoover roundup sent over **one million Mexican illegal aliens packing**—freeing up jobs for out-of-work US citizens. In addition, some <u>47 thousand Mexican nationals who were in the country legally, with visas, also opted to leave</u> due to rising animosity by out-of-work Americans for any foreigner in the United States with a job. *Operation Wetback* was launched in the Southwest: Arizona, California, New Mexico and Texas. But deportees also came from Colorado, Illinois, Michigan, and New York. Since Mexican illegals tried hard to remain under the radar screen, few of them traveled far beyond the border States, thus we can assume that most of the deportees from the States north of the Mason-Dixon line were legal residents. During the Hoover years, <u>immigration to the United States was virtually stopped</u>. The Hoover deportations caused an outcry from the Mexican government demanding to know what gave Hoover the right to deny Mexican citizens the right to jobs in the United States under what was called the *"Good Neighbor Policy"* set in motion by Woodrow Wilson in 1913. Our President didn't care about his character being mashed in the ground; he worried about putting Americans back to work and increasing the General Welfare. He did what was needed. We can believe the effects were greatly appreciated by Americans, but in the depths of the Great Depression, details of the success are hard to read.

## Roosevelt Opens the Floodgate

By the end of World War II, President Roosevelt had eliminated all the good from Hoover. During these days there were no jobs for US citizens. Unlike Hoover, Roosevelt had been in office to "help" the monster farming masters. Under Roosevelt's Public Law 78 agricultural giants, who needed dirt cheap labor, were allowed to import labor from Mexico even if all immigration quotas had been completely filled. Let me tell you how horrible this law was for the common welfare of Americans. Twenty five percent <u>of the American labor force was still out of work and as much a 70% of the work force was out of work in the farm States while Roosevelt allowed illegals to be shipped in as fast as they could get them.</u> Under Public Law 78, *when work contracts were fulfilled, the employer was responsible, under law, to transport the migrant worker back to Mexico.* With no agents recovering the jobs that should have been for the starving Americans, <u>thousands of migrant workers simply vanished into the human landscape, taking what few jobs were available.</u> As one would expect, Roosevelt's hands-off caused <u>illegal alien immigration to increase by 6000%.</u> America was in horrible condition and Truman came along

# Truman [1952]

By 1954, the INS estimated that illegals <u>were again crossing the US border at the rate of one million per year</u>. The INS, as ordered by Harry Truman, went through the motions of rounding up illegal aliens and migrant workers who overstayed their visas. Even with his efforts against the powerful, Truman only was able to deport about 30 thousand Mexicans during his seven years in office so we cannot say he ever read the Constitution or he was afraid to do his duty. The small number of deportations sounds horrible but he did reduce the inrush by something else. Truman was not one for getting illegals out of the country, but he did do something unpopular to some and outside politics as usual to help American's General Welfare called his *Federal Immigration and National Act [1952]*. He was able to push it through in the closing days of his administration. It stated, *"Any US citizen that knowingly assists an illegal alien, provides them with employment, food, water or shelter has committed a felony. City, county or State officials that declare their jurisdictions to be "Open Cities, Counties or States are subject to arrest; as are law enforcement agencies who chose not to enforce this law. Police officers who ignore officials who violate this action are committing a federal felony. If you live in a city, county or State that refuses to enforce the law for whatever reason, the officials making those rules are financially liable for any crime committed within their jurisdiction by an illegal alien."* This would be all that Eisenhower needed.

# Eisenhower's Courage [1953]

In keeping with his oath of office and the Constitution, Dwight D. Eisenhower and the Congress of the United States took on this delicate patriotic necessity and removed a very large portion of the illegal aliens. While we didn't have as severe an issue as we do today, it was estimated that 3-million had walked and waded northward over a period of several years with little interference from the previous President, Truman, for jobs in California, Arizona, Texas, and points beyond. It was a mess and people began losing their livelihoods. A Truman-initiated study on Mexican migratory labor in 1950 found that cotton growers in Texas paid migrant workers about half what a US citizen was paid to chop cotton. Eisenhower was stuck will cleaning up the mess created by the open door polices 73rd and 82nd Congresses. As Eisenhower took office, illegal immigrants were now crossing at the rate of about 3 million per year. When Eisenhower assumed the Oval Office, illegal alien migration was one of his top priorities. He attributed the lax attitude of Congress about illegal immigration with a relaxation of Congressional ethical standards. As Eisenhower met with current and retired border patrol agents he learned that the big ranchers and farmers who relied on the cheap migrant labor had friends "in high places" in government. Agents were subtlety warned not to arrest the workers employed by what turned out to be powerful campaign donors. When that didn't work, they were very bluntly told to back off, or they were simply transferred where they would become someone else's problem. President Eisenhower knew what the Constitution required him to do. He cut off this illegal traffic. He did it quickly and decisively with only 1,075 United States Border Patrol agents. This is less than one-tenth of today's force. The operation is still highly praised among veterans of the Border Patrol. Before Eisenhower became president, the *New York Times* reported on the issue of illegal infiltration. Here is a short excerpt *"The rise in illegal border-crossing by Mexican 'wetbacks' to <u>a current rate of</u> <u>**more** than 1,000,000 cases a year</u> has been accompanied by a curious relaxation in ethical standards extending all the way from the farmer-exploiters of this contraband labor to the highest levels of the Federal Government."* Profits from illegal labor led to the kind of corruption that apparently worried Eisenhower more than most.

It is difficult to estimate the number of illegal aliens forced to leave by Eisenhower's operation in 1953. The INS claimed as many as 1,300,000, though the number officially apprehended was less than this total. The INS estimates concluded that many illegals feared apprehension by the government and voluntarily repatriated themselves before and during the operation. INS agents in the San Antonio district alone, which included most of Texas outside of El Paso, <u>saw an estimated 500,000 to 700,000 fleeing</u> to Mexico just as the campaign began. The whole thing took only 2 years leaving almost all illegals gone.

As I mentioned before, a 1950 study conducted by the President's Commission on Migratory Labor in Texas, showed a 6,000 percent increase in migrant labor and a substantial reduction in wage levels around the southwest.

While this should have scared almost everyone major opposition was pushed by Senators Lyndon B. Johnson (D) of Texas and Pat McCarran (D) of Nevada. They had powerful farm consortium donators and could not allow for American security at the cost of their own power. Luckily General Swing's close connections to the president shielded him and the Border Patrol during this short interval so they could ACTUALLY do their work.

In 1953, before Eisenhower's version of Operation Wetback began, there were over a million workers who had crossed the United States Border illegally. Agricultural works were mostly replaced by cheap "illegal" labor from Mexico with this influx of cheap laborers was an increase in criminality, disease, and illiteracy

The result of Operation Wetback was stunning. Gen. Joseph by early 1954 was capturing illegal immigrants from Mexico. Beginning from the Rio Grande Valley, Wetback spread quickly; illegal aliens were sent back by forced and armed military. On the first day of Operation Wetback, about 5 thousand illegal aliens were "gone". From the day after, about 1,100 illegal aliens were sent back per day. The United States government had shown that they would not tolerate illegal activities that would reduce Constitutional general welfare of Americans. Let me show you a fairly simple chart concerning Eisenhower's efforts. It's called the Nonfinancial Corporation Labor share.

What you seen in the chart is that Eisenhower's operation wetback increased this labor factor by about 6% from 1953 until 1955 and after a short recession it rebounded to about the same level until his Presidency had ended. Once the Kennedy/ Johnson reign started there was massive pressure on the job market 1966 that did not recover until about 1970 when Nixon took control of the United States. You may notice that since GW Bush became president and through the Obama reign this number has been steadily decreasing while money spent on welfare has been skyrocketing.

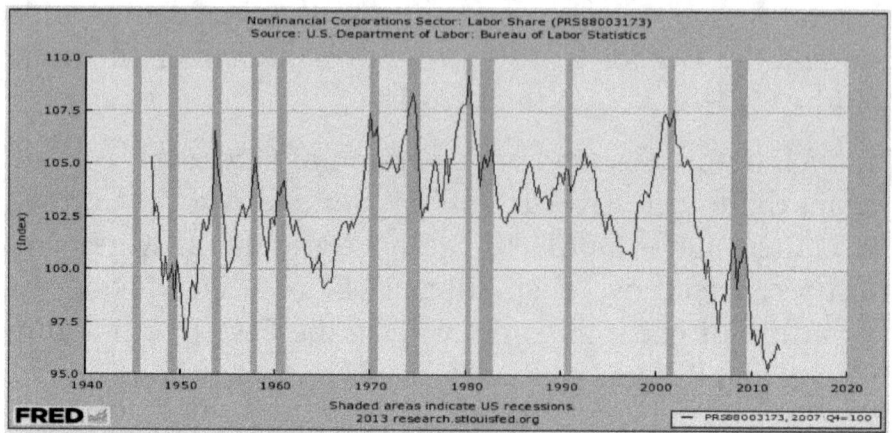

Another unemployment chart shows a marked reduction in joblessness of Americans as the Illegal Aliens were exported [2% reduction to 4%] and the unemployment reduction stayed low throughout most of his term.

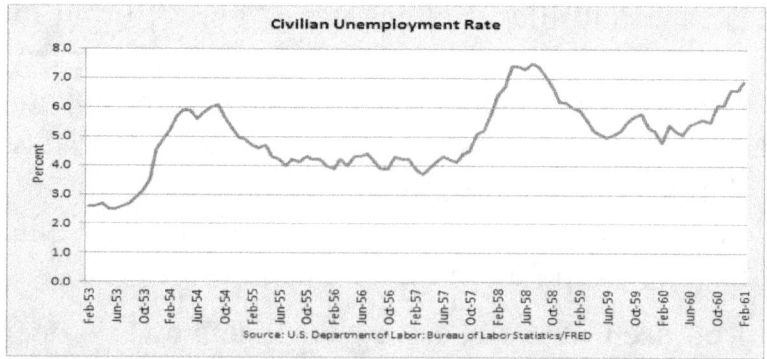

Let me show you one more chart. The following Chart from the Beareau of Labor Statistics data shows percentage of Americans working from 1950 until 1976 and the participation percentage of Americans in the workforce averaging around 60%, but notice something important as we look at what happened after Eisenhower's elimination of Illegal's in 1954. People took the jobs left by the illegals in record numbers causing a huge jump the reduction of unemployed of Americans as you would expect. Don't let someone tell you Amercians will not take menial jobs. We can assume the same thing happened after the similar action taken by President Hoover, but that data is unavailable.

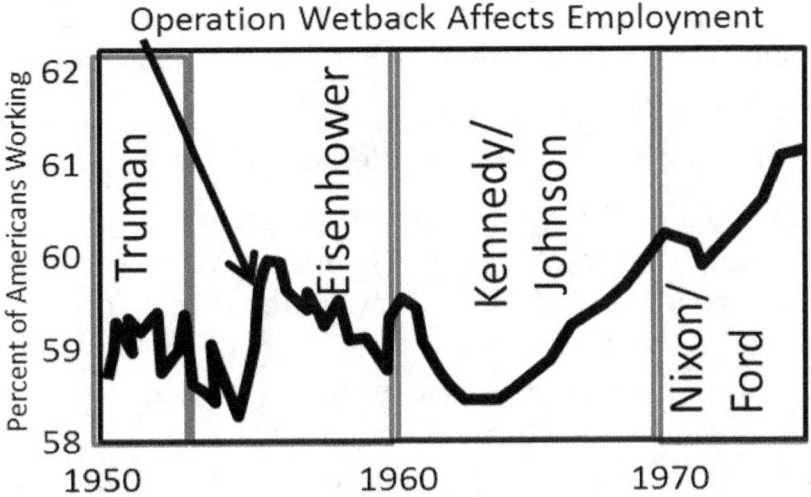

# Since Eisenhower

We find failure after failure to protect Americans and assure reasonable welfare to Americans. Instead of discouraging and preventing illegals form assaulting our country, 4 Presidents did the opposite and encourage, allowed, praised, and comforted . Presidents Reagan, Clinton, and Obama. The anti constitution actions seem horrible, but they were done anyway.

## Reagan's Challenge to Welfare of Americans

In 1986, <u>under Reagan</u>, Congress passed the Immigration Reform and Control Act (IRCA) which gave amnesty to all illegal aliens who had evaded law enforcement for at least four years **or** who were working illegally in agriculture. Isn't that or a strange one? He allowed the illegals who had been convicted of crime be Americans if they were agricultural workers!!! This resulted in **2.8 million illegal aliens** being admitted as legal immigrants to the United States.  As one would expect, unemployment would have had a quick increase as "registered Jobs now showed up. Unfortunately, the job market stayed the same even with substantial efforts to create new jobs. The misery of the "normal Americans" was not reduced when those 2.8 million jobs could have been much better used.

## Clinton's Challenge to Welfare of Americans

Clinton continued his efforts to reduce American jobs in "The Amnesty of 1994" – This was supposed to be a "temporary" rolling amnesty for **578,000 illegal aliens**. In 1997 he made another "temporary" extension *"The Extension Amnesty of 1997"* but that wasn't enough. *"The Nicaraguan Adjustment and Central American Relief Act Amnesty of 1997"* and **another million** would be converted to Americans and encourage many more to infiltrate our country. Another encouragement for illegal trafficking of people to Americans was Clinton's *"Haitian Refugee Immigration Fairness Act Amnesty of 1998"* which converted **another 125,000 illegal aliens**. He then decided to continue the horror as the illegal aliens would become Americans even though there was no way to absorb these people without reducing the standard of living of many Americans. Next came the *"Late Amnesty of 2000"*. This was an amnesty for almost ½ million illegal aliens who claimed they should have been amnestied under the 1986 IRCA amnesty. He did stop and came up with the *"LIFE Act Amnesty of 2000"*. This was a reinstatement of the rolling Section 245(i) amnesty to convert **about a million more** to reduce the per-capita wealth of our nation and reduce job opportunity for Americans.

### President Bush's Horror

President Bush didn't call it amnesty, but in 2004 he established the *"Guest Worker Alien Plan"*. Really an amnesty for illegal aliens, it has been determined that it alone caused at least a 15% to 25% increase in illegals entering the United States. Remember, by showing others they need not worry about the limitations on people who could infiltrate our land, many others followed.

### President Obama's Horror

Last but not least, this president ordered the entire justice function of our country to ignore all illegals and even help them come into our country. Millions have entered and the rate is expanding under his watch as his quasi-amnesty of ignoring has done its worst.

*An amnesty is a reward to those breaking the law. Issuing an amnesty to illegal aliens only encourages more illegal immigration into the United States.*

After the 1986 amnesty, illegal immigration increased significantly. Census Bureau 2000 data indicate that 700,000 to 800,000 illegal aliens settle in the U.S. each year, with somewhere between 12 and **40 million** illegal aliens now currently living in the United States.

*Amnesty benefits neither our society nor those being amnestied.*

The only thing you can be assured of with this huge population of illegal aliens is crime. According to the Immigration and Naturalization Service, the average illegal alien had only a seventh-grade education and earned less than $9,000 a year [EVEN IF HE HAD BEEN AMESTIED] The only difference is that it was easier for them to get additional welfare. According to the *Center for Immigration Studies,* the cost of the 1986 IRCA amnesty alone was over $78 billion in the ten years following the amnesty. That is Billion with a "B" and we can certainly believe this is a substantial understatement.

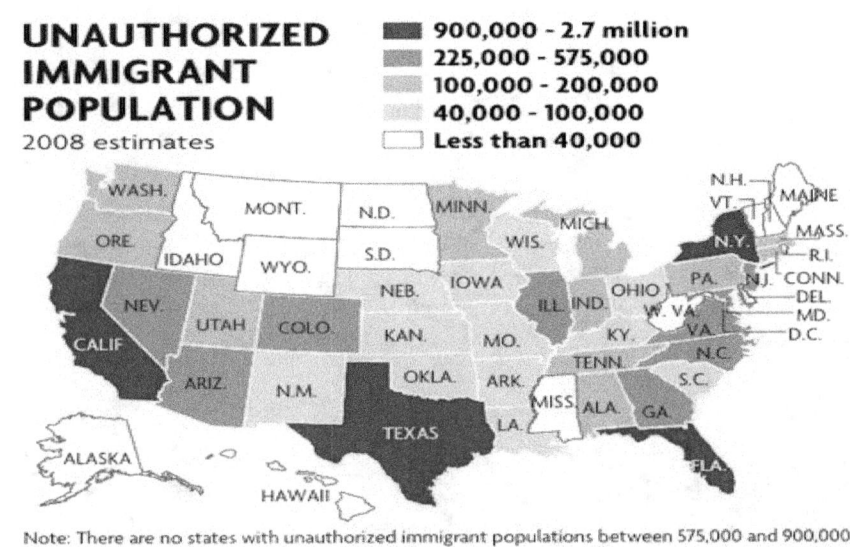

**UNAUTHORIZED IMMIGRANT POPULATION**

2008 estimates

- 900,000 - 2.7 million
- 225,000 - 575,000
- 100,000 - 200,000
- 40,000 - 100,000
- Less than 40,000

Note: There are no states with unauthorized immigrant populations between 575,000 and 900,000

Source: Pew Hispanic Center

NEWS STAFF/JODY POTTER

As the preceding map shows, in 2008 there were over 2 million illegal aliens living in Florida, in Texas, in California, and in New York. Besides those there were 9 States with about ½ million each and another 21 have about 100 thousand or more. These numbers have risen significantly, but a general map shows concentration of those reducing our General Welfare.

While no one should use the term immigration when discussing illegal criminals, the following chart shows the estimated costs to each state because of these unregistered aliens who should not be here. The chart comes from the Federation for Immigration Reform who found that $84 Billion has been spent by taxpayers each year to subsidize these intruders. A lot of people could be put back to work for $84 billion every year.

## Things to Address

1. There is no question that removing the Illegals will reduce joblessness.

2. There is no question it will make our country safer.

3. There is n question that it has been done 2 times before so there is NO coConsititutional issue no matter what anyone says.

4. In many ways it is political suicide to do what Eisenhower and Hoover did, but that does not mean it shouldn't be done.

5. Ther is no question that the $84 billion a year spent protecting the Illegal aliens would go a long way at making all Americans more comfortable by creating a huge number of jobs.

# Establish Jobs not Slavery

Even if we start to control, limit, reduce and eliminate illegal entry of foreigners that exceed the quotes set to protect us, we still have another serious problem that limits and generally eliminates any action to provide the General Welfare that is something we can call the establishment of government slavery and more and more become totally dependent on the government.

### How can we Eliminate this Slavery?

One thing to do is we must eliminate the *Earned Income Credit*, free day care, free housing, free lunch, free food stamps, free phones, and free medical handouts as they are currently established. I'm certainly not saying we should not provide those funds to insure domestic tranquility and reduction in lawlessness as required in the Constitution, but the funds cannot be given to those not working. Instead, welfare payments MUST be given to industry in some way with the stipulation and restriction that funds are for hiring those not working and to allow for a low-cost workforce to be trained. This could be done by tax credit, earned income credit to a company, or many things that would not even cost up-front money. I know it sounds simple, but there would not be as many kickbacks so someone would truly need to make a pledge to govern in accordance to our Constitution rather than the corrupt form we have let ourselves accept.

This redistribution of "welfare dollars" would allow free or nearly free **American Manpower** from people who are desperately trying to find work and push themselves towards freedom. By not being enslaved by the government directly the system would build confidence, establish a place of learning, generate more community awareness, build country patriotism, and ---over time—allow those needing opportunity to pursue liberty that goal and vision while REDUCING the cost of supporting our population.

*By working for the money, they spend on medical, food, daycare, housing, and survival, these Americans can begin to increase their confidence, increase pride in their country, increase possibility of sustained livelihood away from government assistance and a large portion will soon be on their own if the program was run in an appropriate way.*

The chart below shows how Roosevelt's stuff began a huge cost in what we now call welfare payments. Notice that when Truman got elected, just about all these things were eliminated. When Johnson came into power we began a spiral of death and we began losing the war on poverty in something he laughingly called the "War on Poverty".

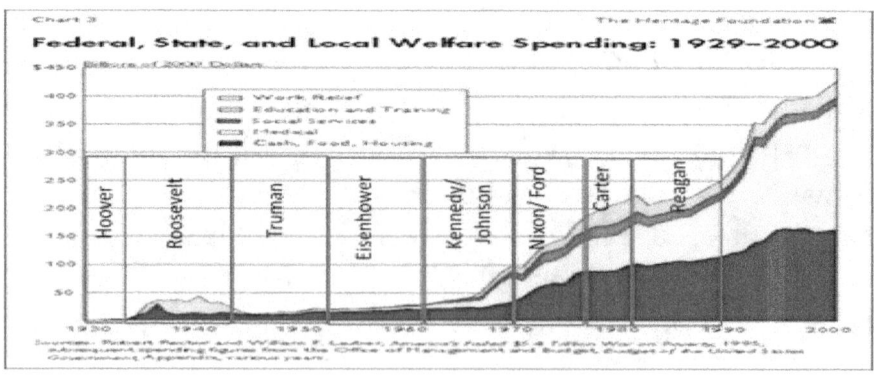

# Eliminate Glamorized Poverty

On a similar note, we must eliminate the glamorization of poverty. Given 2 choices getting money for nothing or getting money for work, some will pick the first one. OK!

*Many will as we see every day as there is no stigma for not working.*

There is no stigma for poverty for poverties sake at all. Those on food stamps buy almost any type of food they want. Certainly, minimum daily food substance should be provided, especially to children, but the food should be provided by rigid adherence providing most of this support by leftover food stuff, and mass quantity cereals that provide this limited subsistence without the desire for poor to use this program to buy expensive steaks or put their families on food stamps to cover their smoking, drinking, or drug habits. These things are becoming an encouragement to not work. They allow desperate people to slip into the Slavery of the welfare State.   Some indicate we cannot embarrass the poor and I believe that is a truth provided they are doing whatever they can to eliminate this state.

I the previous example I presented that showed a woman working part time at $29,000 per year made more money that a woman making $69,000 per year if both had 2 children to care for. There is a certain glamor to that whole thing--the life of "freedom from work". Instead of paying direct payments to provide this same service, wouldn't it be better to provide funding to an industry so the poor woman could have a decent full time job and training for some time, bring her up to something near the $69,000 wage for a time, have her pay for those things she needs and not give the other mother a slap in the face for working full time to take care of her family?

## Discouraged from Finding Work

If you want to jeopardize our General Welfare the most, simply discourage people from finding work. Bringing in foreigners to work to limit jobs not only reduces the jobs available, but also limits jobs by artificially increasing salaries of second tier jobs so that only those well qualified can get them. I know this sounds backwards, but even while jobs are fading those in technical positions still are doing well. There are at least almost 100 different federal programs designed to *"help" lower-income* Americans as shown below. The problem is they all do the opposite eliminate freedom, reduce our workforce and stifle the welfare of our country.

| Program Area | # of federal programs | Cost in FY2012 |
|---|---|---|
| Cash aid | 5 | $250 billion |
| Education and job training | 28 | $100 billion |
| Energy | 2 | $5 billion |
| Food aid | 17 | $150 billion |
| Health care | 8 | $300 billion |
| Housing | 22 | $50 billion |
| Social Services | 8 | $15 billion |
| Veterans | 2 | $25 billion |
| TOTALS | 92 | $1 trillion |

There are dozens of education and job-training programs which could help if they were run right. There are 17 different food-aid programs and over 20 housing programs. The federal government spent about a $trillion on these programs in fiscal year 2014. Just imagine what a $trillion dollars could do for our country in ACTUALLY establishing the GENERAL Welfare. If we just take the money spent over the last 50 years since Johnson's failed *"war on poverty"* supposedly was started, U.S. taxpayers have spent over $22 trillion on the anti-constitutional promote-poverty programs. Let me give you a comparison.

*Once adjusted for inflation, this spending (not including Social Security or Medicare) is three times the cost of all U.S. military wars since the American Revolution.*

- **The Social Security Amendments of 1965-** created Medicare and Medicaid and also expanded Social Security benefits for retirees, widows, the disabled and college-aged students, financed by an increase in the payroll tax cap and rates.

- **The Food Stamp Act of 1964**, which made the food stamps program a permanent addition to the increase in poverty.

- **The Economic Opportunity Act of 1964.** This thing established the Job Corps, the VISTA program, the federal work-study program and a number of other initiatives. All failed, but no one even tried to fix them.

- **The Head Start Program-** was another 1965 fiasco, but no one seemed to address it that way and poverty continued to skyrocket and more and more money was being paid to non-workers.

- **The Elementary and Secondary Education Act**, signed into law in 1965, subsidizing school districts with a large share of impoverished students. This stupid thing has been changed to something called *"No Child Left Behind Act"*. This actually should be called ALL CHILDREN LEFT BEHIND as passing school classes now does not require learning so the poor stay poor.

The sad facts are that today, 4 million Americans are not consider poor because they are paid food stamps as shown below which now costs our country almost $50 billion a year and rising at an unbelievable, out-of-control rate.

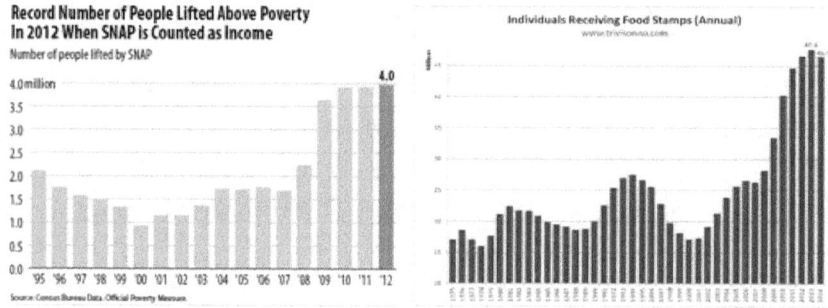

### The glamor shows how we now view poverty

Here is a sad fact. According to government surveys, the typical family that is identified as poor has air conditioning, cable or satellite TV, and a computer in his home. Forty percent have a wide screen HDTV and another 40 percent have internet access. Three quarters of the poor own a car and roughly a third have two or more cars.

### Poverty Rise

According to OPM [official poverty measures], overall poverty rates increased from only 14 percent in 1967 to 15 percent in 2012 which is totally horrible, is not even near the truth as so much money is being pumped into the poor to make it look like they are not poor it just makes you sick. The supplemental data eliminating the artificial offsets show the poverty rates are nearly double [18% to 33%].

- Slavery producing 'Earned income Credits' alone **made it appear** that 6.7 million people were not in what has been called the poverty level or 5%.

- Slavery producing Child Tax Credit is said to have **artificially reduce poverty** level numbers by something like 10%.

- Slavery producing measures expanded Social Security.

- Slavery producing Food Stamps **artificially reduced poverty** numbers by 4%

- Slavery producing housing subsidies also have contributed to this **fake anti-poverty push**.

The chart below shows the official poverty rate, the explosion of government enslavement money being pushed and the poverty increase minus this massive fake money that forces people into the enslavement of poverty.

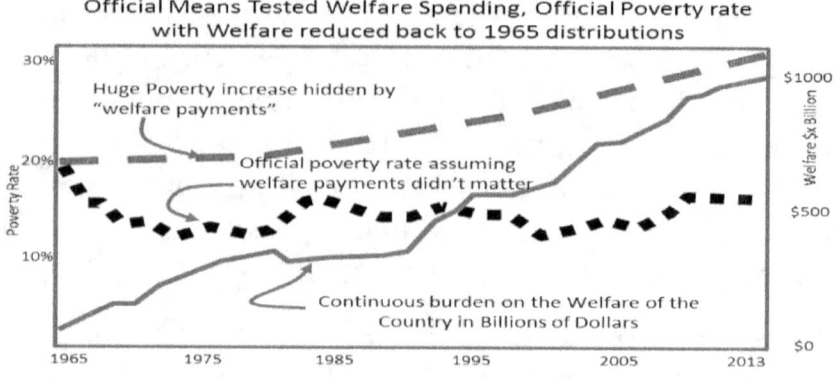

Official Means Tested Welfare Spending, Official Poverty rate with Welfare reduced back to 1965 distributions

Huge Poverty increase hidden by "welfare payments"

Official poverty rate assuming welfare payments didn't matter

Continuous burden on the Welfare of the Country in Billions of Dollars

# Slow the Welfare Spiral

We must also reduce population of continuation. I am sorry to say, some people who cannot provide for themselves have offspring that they cannot provide for. There has to be a way to halt this spiral. One possibility is that welfare payments or subsistence must have a price. While having a child on subsistence should always be allowed, it seems only practical that a second child should not be permitted. If someone tries to continue, all payments SHOULD be removed. One thing that is apparent. If a mother can have a child as she is able to take on that effort, she certainly could be working.

**No Father**

A second issue is the separation of family cause by current slavery methods. If a man claims his family, taxes are increase, welfare payments are decrease or eliminated, and fathers are removed from the lives of their children. We must eliminate this issue. Certainly, the work for money method will help, but there should not be a penalty for being married, in fact, a woman should always be required to identify the father and no funding for support should be established until AFTER the father is contacted and support is established in some way. The payment for work instead of free money and services will help here as well. More people will stay together and with more fathers heading families, crime will be reduced.

Indeed, the single biggest accomplishment of the War on Poverty seems to have been the proliferation of single parent households and children being born out of wedlock. In 1964 the percentage of American children born to unwed mothers was approximately 4%. Today the figure has skyrockets to 800% of that number. According to studies by HHS and others, that's largely because the welfare state has made such a choice not only feasible but preferable. Here is what they said.

*Holding constant a wide range of variables, including income, education, and urban vs. suburban setting, the study found that a 50 percent increase in the value of AFDC and food-stamp payments led to a 43 percent increase in the number of out-of-wedlock births.*

# Reduce Incarceration

It has been determined that a majority of those in our prisons today came from broken homes. Our nation must encourage a strong family life rather than forcing its limitation. The following chart shows the massive increase in incarcerated Americans since the War on Poverty began.

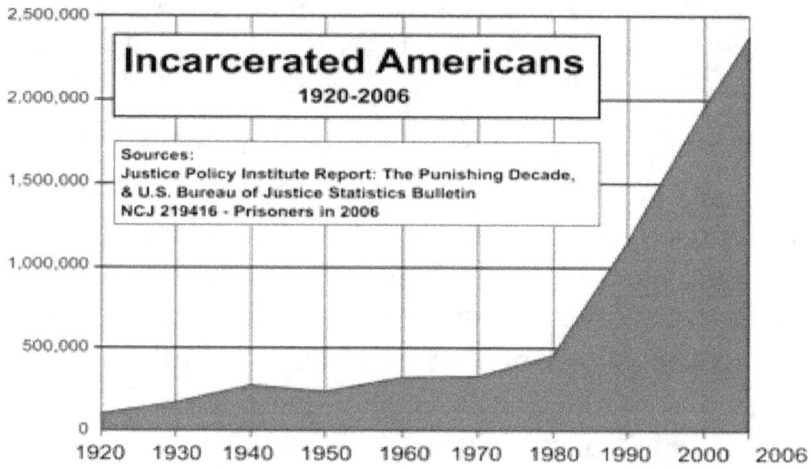

Here is what we read from the "Atlantic Magazine".

*"The relationship [between single-parent families and crime] is so strong that controlling for family configuration erases the relationship between race and crime and between low income and crime. This conclusion shows up time and again in the literature."*

In 1965 when the "war on poverty" or the "war to enslave the poor" there were 20 violent crimes for every 1000

Americans. By 2013 that number was almost double. Now for the real truth; the population has tripled during that time so the statistic is that there are 6 times as many violent crime inmates today as the General Welfare is again disregarded. Not only is this violence caused by reduced families, but also the huge reduction in pride of one's self obtained by working for a living. Let's say this once more.

*Since Johnson War Toward Poverty, violent criminals have increased by 600 percent.*

# Instill Patriotism

If there is no patriotism, pride in country above other countries, there will soon be no country. One might ask, "How do we increase patriotism in a land divided by poverty and ethnicity?" The answer is to reduce poverty and Identity of ethnicity, and push out any socio-communistic backdrop. All are difficult but they can be accomplished if Congress and the President want to go back to the Constitution and actually provide for General Welfare and the pursuit of liberty. Most don't have a desire to save our country, but we do have the power to elect brave individuals that will go against massive parties run by Unions or Massive companies, or the mindset of communism.

## Eliminate the Socio-communistic Backdrop

Speaking of communism do you know who Saul Alinsky is? You might remember that Hillary Clinton did her thesis on his great works and you might remember that Barrack Obama wrote about him in his own books praising his endeavors, but if you did not say he was a communist, you would be limited in your answer. Alinsky took the Leninist scheme of world conquest and boiled it down for anyone to understand and initiate. It all is focused on the poor. Stalin called the *"Useful Idiots"*. Alinsky had a simple 8-point strategy.

1. **Healthcare**- Control Healthcare and you control the poor.

2. **Poverty**- Increase the poverty level. Poor people are much easier to control and cannot fight if government provides everything for them.

3. **Debt**- Increase the national debt to an unsustainable level. Then you can tax more which will increase poverty [by loss of jobs and loss of income].

4. **Gun Control**- Remove the ability for people to defend themselves from government to allow easy conversion to a police State.

5. **Welfare**- Take control of every aspect of the lives of the poor. [by providing food, housing and income]

6. **Education**- Take control of what people read and listen to and take control of what children learn in school. [So. you can divert truth, instill distrust, bash the non-communistic view, limit knowledge of problems, and reduce patriotism.]

7. **Religion**- Remove God from government and schools. [Without a rudder, all forms of moral attitudes will be diverted and Laissez-faire tolerance to everything will assure the worst will be adopted.]

8. **Class Warfare**- Divide the people into wealthy and poor which will increase discontent and make it

easier to tax the wealth of the wealthy to support the poor.

Halt these things and we will soon go towards a republic. Voltaire said something Appropriate here. He said, *"It is difficult to free fools from the chains they revere."*

## Reduce Poverty

One thing to do is increase jobs. I talked about that already a little but creation of good jobs is a hard one that takes a long time. As I mentioned the first step must be to halt the incessant outlay of slavery making payments from the federal government that restrict desire, eliminate ability of work, and eventually consume many Americans into a self-sustaining poverty trumped up by a Government not caring about the poverty brought on by the Welfare State.

# Reduction in Ethnicity

I know the first thing that comes to mind is have a war. Everyone seems to forget predecessor ethnicity to combat a common demon. That is not recommended. Thomas Jefferson had to say.

> *"A little rebellion now and then is a good thing. It is a medicine necessary for the sound health of government. God forbid that we should ever be twenty years without such a rebellion."*

 What he was talking about was that complacency was the harbinger of failure in a country. The more people with secondary loyalties away from our country increase complacency. We must fight to ensure country pride is not replaced by ethnic pride.

### Ethnic Diversity Must be Controlled

I already discussed the requirement to limit influx of foreign ideas and people to tolerable levels so that job growth can help Americans first and foreigners only when needed but there is another thing to consider here. We must immerse foreigners into Americanism rather than diversion. One way is to require American speech as much as possible. Those wishing to become Americans should not have a difficult test, but it certain should only be given in English and require written test verification. I know that sounds harsh again, but we MUST increase patriotism in the

United States rather than having a population divided by ethnic boundaries. Let me tell you something that is going to make you sick.

The Obama administration is ordering the nation's public schools remove this patriotic mindset and establish a haven for those not immersed in our society and illegally residing in our country even when job levels are extremely low and 60% or our American youth are without any job. Schools are being REQUIRED to *"support illegal immigrants, and embrace and value the diversity and cultural backgrounds of the foreigners"*. He is doing his part by making their education paid by American taxpayer-funded education. If a student discloses that he or she is an illegal immigrant school personnel must now *"convey openness, assurance of confidentiality and establish safe spaces. They must also* address fears of deportation and support the academic success of illegal aliens. They are also required to inform them about financial aid options available under the Deferred Action for Childhood Arrivals (DACA) under which 700,000 illegal aliens have been granted benefits and another 1.5 million are eligible with an expected increase of another ½ Million.

This is no way to instill American pride as there is no reason to transfer one's allegiance at all and allowing the continuation of a foreign language greatly increase the gulf between ethnic groups. Everyone knows this, but many see the unrest as a good thing Let me tell you another horror as I heard on the TV the other day that a Kindergarten was being praised for limiting the amount of English used in their classroom. A full 50% was taught to American and foreign children a different language assured to increase ethnic stress by continuing the biggest gulf between societies [Language difference]. There is absolutely no reason why Americans and those wishing to stay in America should not be forced to use English to some level. If they want to hold onto the patriotic desire for a different country they WILL NOT HELP HERE.

# Reduce Monopolies to Control Greed

Enough of the identification, care, and return of American to the workforce and instilling patriotism, we must simultaneously reduce artificial cost inflators. One to be looked at here is something we call monopoly or oligopoly [few controllers of an entire industry]. While many monopolies are hidden some even are allowed to operate out in the open and restriction of conglomeration laws have been reduced and eliminated over the last 50 years. Two that we can quickly realize are the monopolies of Hospitals and Pharmaceutical conglomerates. Don't get me wrong, we could pick a number of monopolized industries, but these are the most abusive so let's investigate how we might help America. By the way do not even believe that because there are 3 or 4 major pharmaceutical companies and a number of seemingly separate hospitals all catering to the will of the AMA [most powerful union in the United States] that these are not monopolies. Just try to go to another company to buy some fancy drug only one company designed. Just try to get a hospital action for the same price as the world market dictates. Many drug companies are so ashamed of the cost of an American drug that they provide the same drug to a foreigner for ----wait for it---- LESS than the country that paid for the research.

*Today, Americans are in trouble. <u>Medical processes here cost 2 times</u> that of the rest of the world and don't believe it is because we have better medicine and a higher level of living.*

This is simply not so, in fact, many of those requiring drugs and hospitals are the poorest people in our country. We hide the issue with things like Medicare, Medicaid, and Insurance, but this monopoly will soon destroy us if it continues unrestrained. Somehow there must be given a "restriction of service price" for this almost excusive corporation or labor union of Doctors, Pharmaceuticals, and Hospitals. Certainly, this horror is one that is being hidden by insurance only to be removed when our pain is greatest, but the whole thing is totally opposite the requirement of our government to assure "GENERAL WELFARE" of Americans.

There could easily be a comparative pricing of services around the world to establish a level of price control. Don't think of price control as a bad thing. Price control is everywhere. When there is a wide enough assortment of possible sources of a product, the common market will regulate the price, but we found out in the 1860 and 70s that a true democracy [one that would not place restriction of greed] cannot work in an environment we people can become greedy. As I mentioned previously this is best noticed in the Medical arena. Let's look at some of the comparisons.

- What you have been told is drug companies need high prices to pay for the huge R&D cost----LIE.

- You were told the USA has the best medicine in the world. ----LIE

- You were told we have more doctors—LIE

- You were told we have more hospital beds for patients. –LIE

- You were told our people are living longer from our high cost medicine. ---LIE

- Drug companies currently are getting "normal profits because of the massive research required. ---LIE

Everything you thought you knew was fabricated. Here are the figures.

**R&D Cost Lie**-For this we look at the actual expenses. They pay between about 10 to 15 percent of their expenses for research, but they use 30 to 40 percent of their incomes for marketing and promotion. Some to think, wait a minute, if we quit the stupid marketing, the price would drop almost in half. One thing to do is eliminate self- prescribing of drugs brought by high cost advertising by not allowing it.

**Profit Lie**- If you look at total drug company profits in a given year, of every retail dollar sale, drug companies get 75 cents PROFIT. This is not normal profit for anything except for a monopoly. They record about 16% profit in general as advertising takes a lot and here is a secret. They almost pay no taxes as they show large R&D expenditures. Therefore, the same drug sold in Canada costs 30% less and it is identical.

**More available Doctors Lie**-There are actually fewer physicians per person than in most other OECD Organization for Economic Co-operation and Development countries. In 2010, for instance, the U.S. had 2.4 doctors per 1,000 people and the average [not the exception for was he OECD average of 3.1.

**More Hospital Bed Lie**-The number of hospital beds in the U.S. was 2.6 per 1,000 population in 2009, lower than the OECD average of 3.4 beds.

**Better Medicine Lie**-Life expectancy in the USA increased by almost nine years between 1960 and 2010. The Average in the OECD countries was 11 and in Japan the increase was 15 years as we fall farther and farther behind in medicine. The average American now lives 78.7 but the world average of 79.8 years shows a horrible statistic.

**USA has more ability to pay lie**- The chart below shows the truth. The United States is 23rd in median wealth of ALL OEDC countries. This is below the half way level as there are only 34 countries that have made it into this club.

| Rating | Country | Net median wealth |
|--------|---------|-------------------|
| 1 | Australia | $ 219,505 |
| 2 | Luxembourg | $ 182,768 |
| 3 | Belgium | $ 148,141 |
| 4 | France | $ 141,850 |
| 5 | Italy | $ 138,653 |
| 6 | United Kingdom | $ 111,524 |
| 7 | Japan | $ 110,294 |
| 8 | Iceland | $ 104,733 |
| 9 | Switzerland | $ 95,916 |
| 10 | Finland | $ 95,095 |
| 11 | Norway | $ 92,859 |
| 12 | Canada | $ 90,252 |
| 13 | Netherlands | $ 83,631 |
| 14 | New Zealand | $ 76,607 |
| 15 | Ireland | $ 75,573 |
| 16 | Spain | $ 63,306 |
| 17 | Denmark | $ 57,675 |
| 18 | Austria | $ 57,450 |
| 19 | Greece | $ 53,937 |
| 20 | Sweden | $ 52,677 |
| 21 | Germany | $ 49,370 |
| 22 | Slovenia | $ 44,932 |
| 23 | United States | $ 44,911 |

**We pay about the same actually-Lie**-From this level of poverty, we pay2.5 times as much as the average OEDC country as depicted below from 2012 data.

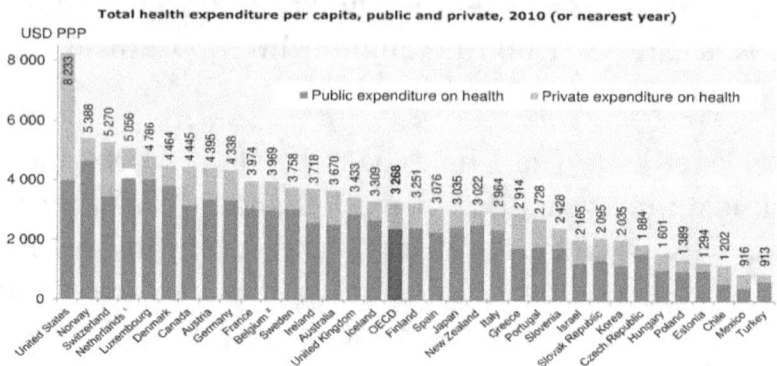

Total health expenditure per capita, public and private, 2010 (or nearest year)

**Everyone comes to America for Medicine Lie**- The second chart below shows which countries are doing the most care per 1000 people. In almost all cases we are not the best.

| | United States | Rank compared with OECD countries | OECD average |
|---|---|---|---|
| MRI units | 31.6 per million population | 2nd | 12.5 per million population |
| MRI exams | 97.7 per 1 000 population | 2nd | 46.3 per 1 000 population |
| CT scanners | 40.7 per million population | 3rd | 22.6 per million population |
| CT exams | 265.0 per 1 000 population | 3rd | 123.8 per 1 000 population |
| Tonsillectomy | 254.4 per 100 000 population | 1st | 130.1 per 100 000 population |
| Coronary bypass | 79.0 per 100 000 population | 3rd | 47.3 per 100 000 population |
| Knee replacements | 226.0 per 100 000 population | 1st | 121.6 per 100 000 population |
| Caesarean sections | 32.9 per 100 live births | 6th | 26.1 per 100 live births |

**Only certain procedures are expensive in USA LIE**- The chart below shows that the United States is the exclusive winner in taking advantage of the population.

**(US dollars, 2007)**

| Procedures | AUS | CAN | DEU | FIN | FRA | SWE | USA |
|---|---|---|---|---|---|---|---|
| Appendectomy | 5 044 | 5 004 | 2 943 | 3 739 | 4 558 | 4 961 | 7 962 |
| Normal delivery | 2 984 | 2 800 | 1 789 | 1 521 | 2 894 | 2 591 | 4 451 |
| Caesarean section | 7 092 | 4 820 | 3 732 | 4 808 | 5 820 | 6 375 | 7 449 |
| Coronary angioplasty | 7 131 | 9 277 | 3 347 | 5 574 | 7 027 | 9 296 | 14 378 |
| Coronary artery bypass graft | 21 698 | 22 694 | 14 067 | 23 468 | 23 126 | 21 218 | 34 358 |
| Hip replacement | 15 918 | 11 983 | 8 899 | 10 834 | 11 162 | 11 568 | 17 406 |
| Knee replacement | 14 608 | 9 910 | 10 011 | 9 931 | 12 424 | 10 348 | 14 946 |

# Coming out of Recession

Some balk at the notion that our country is dying. Just this year, in 2015, we are told our unemployment rate has tapped out and is seeing a reduction while our massive trust to give the poor more money so the standard of living goes up and the poor fall farther into the slavery of Government welfare payments that are taken away if someone dares to get a job. According to contorted bookkeeping unemployment is down to 5.1% which is a drop of 5% over the past 6 years. Just saying it makes my leg tingle. It sounds too good to be true----and so it is.

We need to look at something called underemployment which for example having someone with a college degree waiting tables for lack of any reasonable opportunities for a person with their educational qualifications. This taking of the menial jobs forces others out of work and destitute so how can someone say the unemployment is lower. The answer is anyone not receiving unemployment benefits is no longer counted as being American. They are simply the poor festering in poverty as substance money is poured down from the federal government to keep them quiet. Another thing happening is that many employers are being forced to only allow workers to work 30 hours a week to keep from having to pay the onerous Obamacare government supported medical.

## Labor Participation Rate [LPR]

While not describing underemployed or those only able to work part-time, there is an indicator that helps us see the true unemployment. What we see is there are now 100 million Americans over the age of 16 that are not working. The Obama Administration keeps running out the deceit that this is because of all the baby boomers retiring. The fact is that the labor force participation rate for the age group 16 to 24 **is only 55.1%.** That is a reduction of over 10% from 66% during the 1990's. It is also down over 5% (60.8%) from 2005. Sure, myopic minimum wage increases are harming the employment of this age group with the least work experience, but that is not the total explanation. The Obama manipulation gets worse because the LPR is lower for the prime working years of 25-54 years old. In 2000 the LPR for this age group was almost 85%. It was down to 83% when the recession started, but has now plummeted to 80.7%. It is clear the baby boomers are not the only source of reduction in the LPR and it is clear there are no new jobs of any consequence. You may wonder why this is such a big deal. The LPR for September 2015 was 62.4%. That is 3.7% less than August, 2005 exactly ten years earlier; if you review the Department of Labor statistics you see virtually unstopped monthly decline in the LPR during the entire Obama Presidency. Even after the last recession was determined to have gone, the LPR has steadily declined another 3.3%. The chart below shows how the number of workers is being reduced as the fake unemployment reduction try to show a false sense of security.

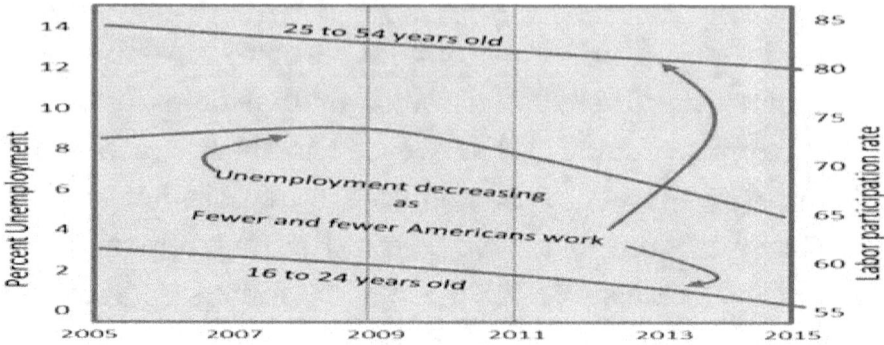

To make these figures worse, we know that more and more seniors are working longer to compensate for inadequate retirement savings. To put a value to the 3.7% figure, at least 12 million more people would be working today if we had the same LPR as ten years ago and remember, this does not include the just barely making it part time and those taking lesser jobs. Instead these 12 million have been added to the subsistence poverty slaves. A cynical person would say the fact that more people are receiving government benefits is the driver behind the reduction in people participating in the labor force. As more become enslaved we come closer to losing our country.

Let me back up a little and talk about the opposite issue where Industry gets so powerful hiring people for less and less that soon, people become enslaved to their work. This will also destroy our country and almost did. The reason our country almost died 50 years ago was something called simple GREED.

# Control Greed

Some may wonder if there is anything that can be done about greed. The answer is that while a country cannot survive as an economically thriving socialist or communistic State, it cannot survive long as greed-controlled Country established under an uncontrolled-democracy. The only sustaining government that can thrive for long periods is a republic that controls greed by establishing limits from monopolies and oligopolies. Our country almost was destroyed in the mid-1800s while 33 people became richer than almost anyone because of the unleashed power of greed, monopoly, and abandonment of consciousness. These anti-Americans caused one of our worst wars, raped the American public with catch phrases like manifest destiny, and Industrial Revolution to hide the corruption paid for by freedom to monopolize an industry like medicine governed by a single doctor's union or hiding behind an unrestricted Patent law or smoothed over by special deals between insurance companies and hospitals. The big monopolies of the mid 1800s were in railroads and oil. The following list shows some of the more well-known multi-billionaires who controlled most of the money and Congress in America. Industry controlled the United States during this time and the only reason we survived through the worst of it was the leaving of

Americans from cities towards the west. Today we cannot move west so monopolies MUST be controlled with more stringent anti-trust laws, more open pricing, and more pride in America. We must become a Republic again. I know Bill Gates [number 4 in the list] didn't get his money during this horrible time, but he is an exception.

| Rank | Name of Industrialist | Birth/ death dates | Source of wealth | Estate $B |
|---|---|---|---|---|
| 1 | John D. Rockefeller | 1839-1937 | oil | 190 |
| 25 | Henry H. Rogers | 1840-1909 | oil | 25 |
| 26 | Oliver Hazard Payne | 1839-1917 | oil | 25 |
| 38 | William Rockefeller | 1841-1922 | oil | 17 |
| 2 | Andrew Carnegie | 1835-1919 | steel | 101 |
| 3 | Cornelius Vanderbilt | 1794-1877 | railroads | 96 |
| 9 | F Weyerhaeuser | 1834-1914 | railroads | 43 |
| 10 | Jay Gould | 1836-1892 | railroads | 42 |
| 20 | John Blair | 1802-1899 | railroads | 29 |
| 24 | Edward H. Harriman | 1848-1909 | railroads | 25 |
| 27 | Henry Clay Frick | 1849-1919 | steel | 22 |
| 28 | Collis P. Huntington | 1821-1900 | railroads | 22 |
| 33 | Mark Hopkins | 1813-1878 | railroads | 20 |
| 35 | Leland Stanford | 1824-1893 | railroads | 18 |
| 37 | James J. Hill | 1838-1916 | railroads | 17 |
| 5 | Andrew W. Mellon | 1855-1937 | Banking | 32 |
| 5 | Richard B. Mellon | 1858-1933 | Banking | 32 |
| 18 | Moses Taylor | 1806-1882 | banking | 29 |
| 19 | Russel Sage | 1816-1906 | finance | 29 |
| 23 | John P. Morgan | 1837-1913 | Finance | 25 |
| 36 | Hetty Green | 1834-1916 | investing | 17 |
| 11 | Marshall Field | 1834-1906 | Retail | 41 |
| 8 | A.T. Stewart | 1803-1876 | Retail | 47 |
| 16 | James G. Fair | 1831-1894 | gold | 30 |
| 32 | James C. Flood | 1826-1889 | Mine | 20 |
| 17 | William Weightman | 1813-1904 | chemicals | 29 |
| 21 | Cyrus Curtis | 1850-1933 | publishing | 26 |
| 29 | Peter A. Widener | 1834-1915 | streetcars | 21 |
| 31 | Philip D. Armour | 1832-1901 | meatpack. | 20 |
| 34 | Edward Clark | 1811-1882 | Sewing | 18 |

The next cartoons showed the nature of our President during this takeover of the country by these less than honorable men. The President was a puppet for the super, super, super rich and set to crush the Indians. In fact, Lincoln holds the record for number of government sponsored Indian hangings at a single time. In his job as puppet, Lincoln started a massive war.

Almost all Americans were in despair. Many were afraid of him and his mysterious prisons. A New York Magazine, The Old Guard", ran article after article about his hidden prisons, and the hatred the Northern States felt, but the billionaire's club loved him and pulled strings to make him clap.

Sorry for the digression and sorry for making some of you mad so let me get back on topic. One may control greed by controlling monopoly, expanding entrepreneur experience, and limitation by monetary punishment, but there may also be additional ways to insure general welfare rather than the welfare of a select group. I know one could go on and on concerning how greed is breaking down American freedoms just as much as the irresponsible government limiting hope, work, and freedom to all Americans.

Another way to reduce greed is by <u>instilling pride in one's country</u>. Certainly, wars help, but those are awful prices to pay.

# Strange Republic Conversion

While I'm on this subject let's go back to earlier discussion. In the 1870s, massive legislation converted our non-working and broken <u>democracy</u> and turned it into a workable <u>Republic</u> with restrictions on massive companies like Bell Telephone and others. This conversion happened during a time when the men listed previously had raped Americans clean and somehow found a new set of values. Without the aid of them, America would have succumbed to a horrible fate. I know it sounds stupid that a select group of super rich would destroy their hand in the cookie jar and allow America to survive, but that is exactly what they did. Country pride and fear of its loss pushed them into reducing their control, expanding free enterprise, abolishing the monopoly concept, and the beginning of a huge philanthropic push to help America. Carnegie, Rockefeller, Stewart and others gave away multiple $ Billions to help secure freedom "from" their old ways of complete takeover of the country. By assuring reasonable competition, even when government restriction was hindering some expansion, some freedom, and some entrepreneurial endeavor, the American <u>Republic</u> made its way out of almost certain collapse from the horrors of the Aftermath from our 4th Civil War in the United States.

**Uncontrolled Greed Today-**The easiest way to determine greed in any nation is to compare the Mean per-capita wealth with the median. I put together the following chart from the 2010 listing of nation wealth of the 32 OEDC Countries of the world. Those with the largest difference have a <u>huge poverty problem</u> and those with similar numbers have a <u>large middle class</u>. Guess where the United States places? As wealth of the country also plays into poverty, I have taken the Wealth figure and divided it by the poverty ratio to give a listing of the countries with the worst poverty positions. Switzerland is worst followed by the USA. While we have the 5th highest mean per-capita wealth Australia, by far, has the strongest middle class. As shown, USA "Mean wealth figure" is $301K the Median yearly wages are only $45K showing a huge number in the poverty level.

| OEDC country | Mean wealth [$/year] | Poverty % | mean to median | Median wealth [$/Year] | entry wealth level | middle-class Level |
|---|---|---|---|---|---|---|
| Switzerland | 512,562 | 450% | 5.34 | 95,916 | 1 | 9 |
| United States | 301,140 | 230% | 6.71 | 44,911 | 5 | 23 |
| Norway | 380,473 | 183% | 4.10 | 92,859 | 3 | 11 |
| Sweden | 299,441 | 167% | 5.68 | 52,677 | 6 | 20 |
| Denmark | 255,066 | 94% | 4.42 | 57,675 | 9 | 17 |
| Germany | 192,232 | 66% | 3.89 | 49,370 | 16 | 21 |
| Canada | 251,034 | 60% | 2.78 | 90,252 | 10 | 12 |
| Austria | 203,931 | 60% | 3.55 | 57,450 | 15 | 18 |
| Israel | 137,351 | 60% | 3.60 | 38,164 | 21 | 25 |
| Chile | 49,032 | 57% | 4.18 | 11,742 | 27 | 31 |
| Mexico | 35,872 | 55% | 3.69 | 9,718 | 29 | 32 |
| South Korea | 79,475 | 52% | 2.57 | 30,938 | 25 | 26 |
| Czech Rep. | 44,975 | 52% | 2.89 | 15,541 | 28 | 29 |
| Portugal | 89,074 | 50% | 2.29 | 38,846 | 24 | 24 |
| Poland | 26,056 | 50% | 2.86 | 9,109 | 33 | 33 |
| Turkey | 25,909 | 50% | 4.86 | 5,326 | 34 | 34 |
| Hungary | 28,379 | 48% | 2.02 | 14,068 | 31 | 30 |
| Estonia | 33,701 | 47% | 2.14 | 15,724 | 30 | 28 |
| Slovenia | 64,067 | 42% | 1.43 | 44,932 | 26 | 22 |
| Slovakia | 27,224 | 42% | 1.31 | 20,740 | 32 | 27 |
| Ireland | 183,804 | 42% | 2.43 | 75,573 | 18 | 15 |
| Greece | 102,971 | 41% | 1.91 | 53,937 | 23 | 19 |
| Netherlands | 185,588 | 38% | 2.22 | 83,631 | 17 | 13 |
| New Zealand | 182,548 | 37% | 2.38 | 76,607 | 19 | 14 |
| Spain | 123,997 | 36% | 1.96 | 63,306 | 22 | 16 |
| France | 295,933 | 29% | 2.09 | 141,850 | 7 | 4 |
| Iceland | 211,592 | 29% | 2.02 | 104,733 | 14 | 8 |
| UK | 243,570 | 27% | 2.18 | 111,524 | 11 | 6 |
| Japan | 216,694 | 27% | 1.96 | 110,294 | 13 | 7 |
| Australia | 402,578 | 25% | 1.83 | 219,505 | 2 | 1 |
| Luxembourg | 315,240 | 25% | 1.72 | 182,768 | 4 | 2 |
| Finland | 171,821 | 25% | 1.81 | 95,095 | 20 | 10 |
| Italy | 241,383 | 21% | 1.74 | 138,653 | 12 | 5 |
| Belgium | 255,573 | 19% | 1.73 | 148,141 | 8 | 3 |

Some tell you this means we should take from the rich and give to the poor, but that is totally wrong. Instead a republic moderates profit by controlling monopolies, establishing cost controls by world standards, and incentivizes the business owners to get "licence on these restrictions by hiring those desperate for work. The more they help those needing help working, the less restriction.

I know you have heard about this stupid carbon footprint punishment handed out with reguard to putting Americans to work. This is not even close to the type of restrictions

I'm talking about. What is needed is the complete restructuring of monopolistic corporate control, similar to the Fascist State we experienced during and after the 4th Civil War into a welfare defeating Republic.

The Sherman anti-trust must be revitalized, the limitation of banks gambling money on the shock market must be reinstated, the student loan debacle must be eliminated. In place of student loans, work programs can be initiated to allow various manufacturers opportunity to reduce taxes, gain secondary government funding, and help the community almost without cost.

*We must give Industry Incentive to reduce the slavery of Poverty. The federal government cannot do it directly. I will never work.*

What we cannot do is **over tax the rich**.

# Words of Wisdom

For this section, we must go back to the 1950s. Characterization of controlling the rich to satisfy the poor started springing up by communist sympathizers, and an important truth was written into the Congressional Record by congressman Brue Alger who borrowed the words from Gerald L. K. Smith, who had written them in his magazine of that time named, "The Cross and the Flag". Of note Gerald Smith also ran for President as the first candidate from the America First Party in 1944 and lost to Franklin D. Roosevelt just before the important message was penned.

"You cannot legislate the poor into freedom by legislating the wealthy out of freedom. What one person receives without working for, another person must work for without receiving. The government cannot give to anybody anything that the government does not first take from somebody else. When half of the people get the idea that they do not have to work because the other half is going to take care of them, and when the other half gets the idea that it does no good to work because somebody else is going to get what they work for, that my dear friend, is about the end of any nation. You cannot multiply wealth by dividing it."

Let's think about this for a minute. Tax those who can bring jobs to our poor will simply enslave them more and put them even farther from seeing liberty. I don't think there is a way of saying it that can even sound close to being right. What must happen is encouragement for putting people to work and the establishment of rules that will not allow for a monopoly or oligopoly which is about the same as monopoly except 2 or 3 massive companies control a particular market that cannot be well established by varied groups, we must regulate prices to coincide with the rest of the world. It sounds simple, but there are powerful entities that will fight this notion. When I say powerful entities, I don't mean Republican or Democrat powerful; I'm talking about the massive businesses putting the congress and President in power. Besides the Health industries, Banking and stock brokering is followed by massive Military development consortiums, and the massive oil oligopolies.

Another thing we must halt as fast as we can that is punishing industries beyond reasonableness. Punishment to support restriction of an industry or even an individual will certainly hamper production of jobs and the process of reducing the slavery of poverty.

# Limit Punishment

Let me get back to the medical dilemma for a minute. Some may say our medical costs are double because of something called malpractice. The answer is yes. To this end, there needs to be restriction of payouts for accidents, but there also should be consequence. Finding out that 50% of the medical increase is for malpractice, two things must be initiated.

- **Reasonable limits** of payments must be secured by the governments. It is a travesty to see that an insurance company can provide a small portion of a medical bill without issue, but a single individual is billed and hounded for payment many times that expected from large organizations.

- **Doctor punishment Rather than money**-The second thing that should be examined is the doctors having these issues. These problem doctors must have their work scope challenged.

No country can be sustained as an uncontrolled democracy any more than as a communistic enslavement. Controls over frivolous suits must be reduced, but the burdens of the over costed services must be controlled at the same time. Still another horror that limits freedom and the General welfare of our country is the abomination that has become of our schools.

# Fix Our Classrooms

If anyone thinks our country is better off with the concept and issuance of the "*No Child Left Behind Act*", they simply are living under a rock. Our classrooms are being converted from places of learning to places of political correctness, coddling of the minority, punishing those trying to understand, and hating the principles of teaching. Let me give you a simple example.

*Under the "no child left behind" boundaries, a basketball game must use 14 different height hoops so than short children can play, also the fast children must have weights on their legs so the slow ones can play. Worse than that, when the game is over the score must be erased and all children are determined to have the same scores so there is no embarrassment for doing a bad job.*

Some would claim the basketball game would not be fun to watch and the really good players would never become good as there is nothing in it for them. Now multiply this example by thousands and that is what is happening to our children. Instead of instilling pride, self-confidence, and desire to learn as was touted, our children are all losing.

One simple way to determine if there is a problem in our schools is to compare the standings of our schools. What we find is that our school systems are failing in every way. The first chart shows the United State education rating from those that graduated high school and college 40 years ago as compared with how well our schools were doing 10 years ago. The chart shows that the United States is falling fast as our children are losing out by a failed system when compared to the rest of the world.

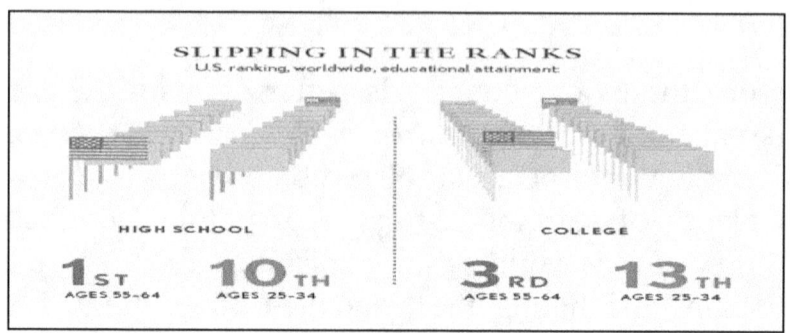

## Rising Costs

This phenomenon is certainly not because we are not spending enough money this broken school system. Look at the horrible results of the next chart. Over the last 80 years with almost no difference in enrolment, reading and math scores have remained the same and science scores have fallen while we have twice as many teachers and spending almost 4 times as much for each student to experience the horror.

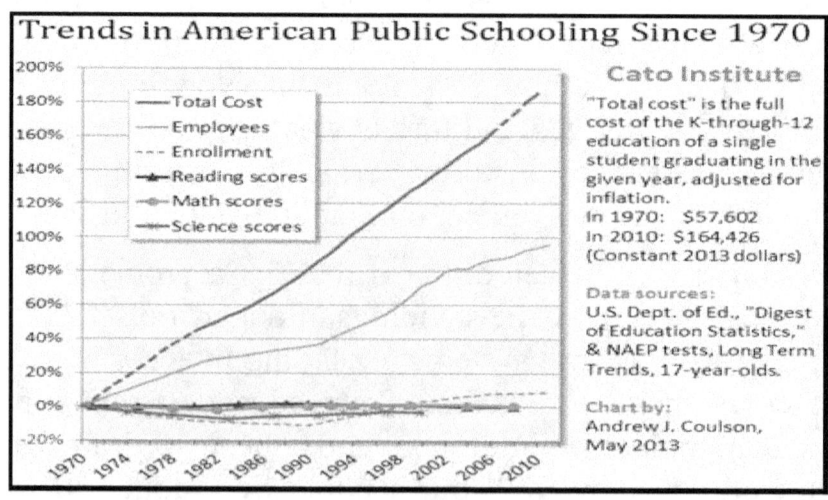

If you are worried, you should be. You could just blame the teachers and say twice as many teachers should be making our schools better, but that is not the problem. The problem is WHAT WE ARE TEACHING. The schools today are not teaching Math, Science, History, Americanism, and honor. They are twisting everything and teaching whatever is most comfortable, whatever assures a student will pass a class, whatever will SEEMINGLY show ethnic and religious tolerance when they are actually pushing Intolerance, Hatred, Bullying, and Segregation of all students. No one can learn in that atmosphere. Hopefully, we can get to the bottom of a number of the issues.

## Lack of Order

To start off, let's look at order. Without order, there can be no learning. One of the reasons for the massive reduction in order and discipline in our schools is the elimination of corporal punishment. While there are still some States that allow corporal punishment to increase order in schools, very little can be done as parents sue schools for "harming" their children. How bogus!!! If we don't get a handle on establishing order in our classrooms, soon we will need high fences around the schools and have to check for weapons at the door. Oh, wait a minute! We already are doing that.

## Everyone Left Behind

Instead of removing disruptive students, someone came up with the law: NO CHILD LEFT BEHIND. What it really means is EVERYONE IS LEFT BEHIND the rest of the world. This has got to stop. Our government is spending substantially more each year and our children are falling farther and farther behind. The next chart shows more teachers per student are being pushed in, but the coddling still reigns supreme so it does no good.

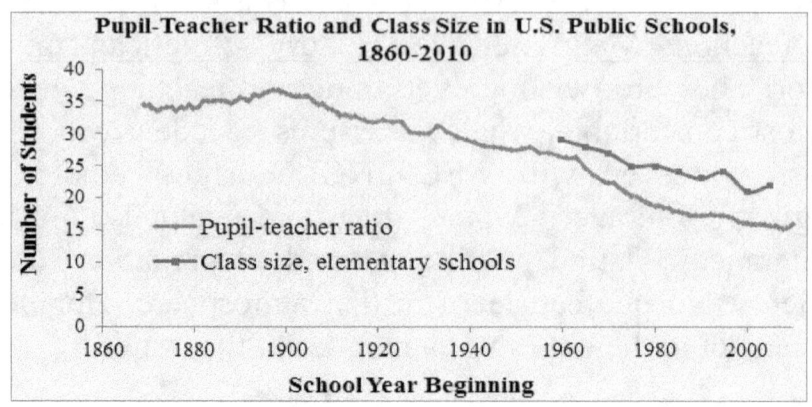

Some think this "No Child Left Behind means the difference between White Black and Hispanic students will be eliminated so all will be able to make a good living. Here is the truth.

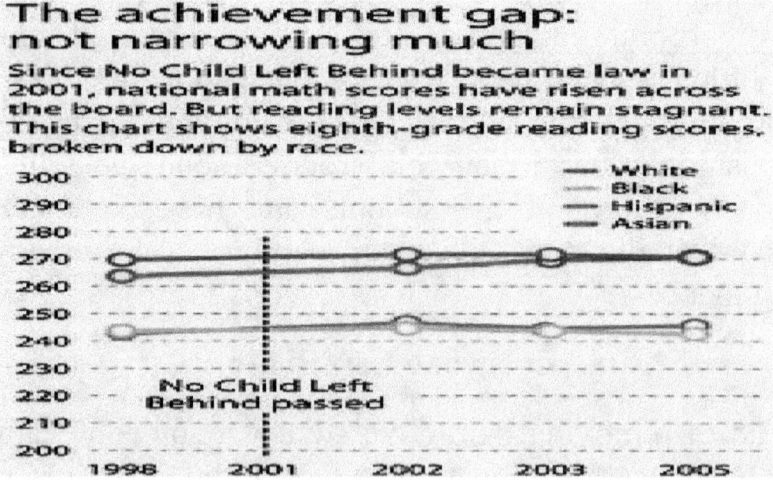

One of the beliefs in this stupid law is that all students will now be educated in learning environments that are safe, drug-free, and conducive to learning. The reality is that 14

percent of eighth graders, 28 percent of 10th graders, and 36 percent of 12th graders used an illicit substance during the past year. By the way; the number of suicides, teen assaults, depression, and undisciplined students has skyrocketed since the leniency of the schools and reduction of corporal punishment. Speaking of undisciplined and unlearned, let's look at a recent college survey.

## College Survey

Recent surveys in colleges asked very difficult questions including:

- *Who is our Vice President?*
- *When was our Revolutionary War?*
- *Who did we fight during that war?*
- *What was the Civil War fought about?*
- *Who won the Civil War?*
- *Who lost the Battle of Little Bighorn?*
- *Cleopatra, was the monarch of what country?*
- *What is the highest mountain range in South America?*
- *What show is Snooky on?*

And many similar questions ----Almost NONE of the college kids knew ANY of the answers. I mean they only knew the last one. No child was finally starting to show results. The next chart shows the remarkable progress of our government push to insure the dumbest student did not feel bad and that the smartest children were simply ignored.

What we are really doing is reducing our children's pride in their country, there capabilities, and their scholastic accomplishments to support a very tiny segment of disruptive, don't want to learn, anti-American, or similar

169

problem children that we do not want to instill discipline, embarrass, or kick out of school. We must halt the incessant disregard for the majority of aspiring Americans to claim religious tolerance, equal opportunity, open mindedness, sexual tolerance, and ethnic tolerance. We should not be tolerant when it tears our country apart.

# Stop Confusing Sex

In this section let me just say that it is estimated the 23 million humans are held in slavery today and most are for sex, with the United States being the one of the top 3 participators of this horrendous form of slavery and debauchery. Instead of focusing on eliminating this sexual deviation, we are being forced by those wanting to take attention off the horrors of someone buying a 7-year-old girl or boy for sex. The things brought up bey the media are things like homosexual deviations, Transvestite deviations, and this new transgender deviation. Please understand that is a tiny group and substantial safeguards are provided for them. Instead of trying to push for men to be able to shower in girl's gym classes, we need to desperately reduce the huge horror of this major sex deviation that is destroying the United States and reducing our collective decency and moral fabric thousands of time worse than a man wanting to wear women's clothes.

The stories you hear of wide satanic perversions on these tiny slaves up to and including sacrificial killings to retrieve this Adrenal chrome stuff is not only true, but much more frequent than any decent person could imagine. It now seems part of the good-life for the Hollywood set includes the Satanic use of sex slaves. It almost makes you want to quit watching TV all together.

> *Our country and our Constitution are established around rule of the majority with <u>tolerance</u> for the minority.*

Sexual deviants are not the majority even if they seem to be the most vocal given this push to hide the real horrors in our country. We should not build our laws around sexual deviations like snake kiss sex disorder victims, dead body lovers, homosexuals, animal sexaholics, Transsexual disorders and the like and we certainly should not allow for the demoralization of our country that was founded on its citizens having <u>inalienable rights</u> given by a God who cannot be happy with us right now.

Here is an idea---anyone who doesn't believe God gives certain inalienable rights because they don't even believe there is a God should not have any of those rights while the rest of us are allowed to hold private property, be able to protect themselves from an onerous government, be heard in a court of law, etc. I'm not saying someone with a homosexual deviation does not believe in God. I'm saying even those without deviant lifestyles who have become secularized cannot expect God given rights.

I know this will get some angry, but this whole concept has been twisted to its breaking point as <u>tolerance</u> has been replaced by <u>glamorization,</u> <u>punishment of normalcy</u>, and <u>forming massive restrictions on the will of the majority</u> to emphasize and glamorize deviations as NORMAL. Let me give you an example.

*The majority of Americans don't go around killing people, but the small minority who do possibly are embarrassed if people didn't consider their actions as normal in our society. If we allowed the minority killers to be thought of an ACCEPTIBLE our society would quickly turn more violent as we glamorized those killing.*

The same holds true for other deviant minority lifestyles. Some would say minorities should not govern a society. Certainly, they should have the rights [within reason] to practice, transsexuality, bestiality, Transvestism, devil incantationism, Bisexuality, Man-boy love, homosexuality, teenage sex and other actions not considered "the norm" by the majority, but the rights of those who deviate from must be constrained and certainly not glamorized. Actions to "normalize" these things confuse sexual response in our children; lead to misguided sexual encounters, establishes less control over morality, and decreases the desire or will to conform to a society. This problem starts small just like all horrors, but *glamorization of deviation* is not the way to enhance the moral fiber of our society. It will only escalate and soon there will be no moral reckoning whatsoever.

Don't give awards to Transsexuals simply for having that deviation unless you want an entire country of Transsexuals. Don't allow special bathrooms for transvestites unless you want Americans to lose understanding of sexual orientation. Let me give you a glimpse of what is happening.

**Gay Lesbian Straight Education Network-**Let's talk about Harry Hay who is called "the father of gay liberation". He fought to have the NAMBLA considered an important part of gay pride. What he said is very telling. *"If the parents and friends of gays are truly friends of gays, they would know from their gay kids that the relationship with an older man is precisely what thirteen-, fourteen-, and fifteen-year-old kids need more than anything else in the world."* This pedophilia stance, promoted by our schools by quiet absolution, is not being stifled at all; in fact, the Gay Lesbian Straight Education Network's (GLSEN's) recommended reading list for kids includes books that depict (and excuse) homosexual encounters between adults and children. In a show of support for this thinking our Boy Scout clubs now are allowing confessed homosexual males to "mentor" very fragile young boys in the ways of life.

**Worsens Every Year-**While the school systems seem to ignore the horrors, the problem of sexual abuse gets worse every year and is 350% worse than it was in 1980.

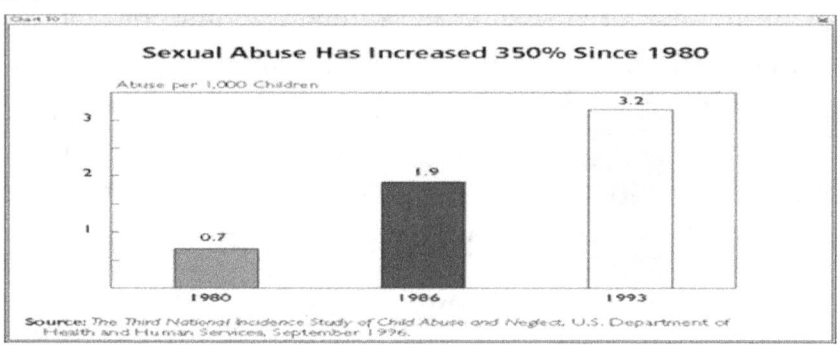

**Sexual Abuse Has Increased 350% Since 1980**

Abuse per 1,000 Children

| | 1980 | 1986 | 1993 |
|---|---|---|---|
| | 0.7 | 1.9 | 3.2 |

Source: *The Third National Incidence Study of Child Abuse and Neglect,* U.S. Department of Health and Human Services, September 1996.

**Federal Office of Civil Rights, Title IX-**Writing on behalf of the NFHS, one of the Massachusetts leaders advises every high school administrator in America that, *"The Federal Office of Civil Rights, Title IX **requires** that boys pretending to be girls, and girls pretending to be boys, must be permitted to compete on, and **share locker room and***

*showering facilities with, the sports teams of the opposite sex.*" [I paraphrased] She further objects, "*Practices such as requiring them to use locker rooms and bathrooms that correspond to their gender assigned at birth discourages participation. The belief that transgender girls are not 'real' girls is sometimes expressed as a concern,*"

**Pornographic Teachers**-Called sex education, this is tearing our scholastic component of schools to pieces as kids are being forced to examine their sexuality, permissiveness, sexual identity, and even their biologic sex as opposed to what they think they should be. Since before 1990, pornographic images like that shown next, demonstrate methods for heterosexual encounters as well and homosexual deviations. The High School instructor below demonstrates anal intrusion for the children so they can go try it.

**Teaching Increased Sexual Activity**-When just looking at sexual activity, the numbers are really bad. The following shows the trend of sexual activity of little 9th graders being subjected to Sex demonstration classes. With fewer classes, in 1991, we see the percentage of children is about 76%. By 2011, the instruction has allowed the activity to increase to 78%. I'm so glad they are teaching this instead of History.

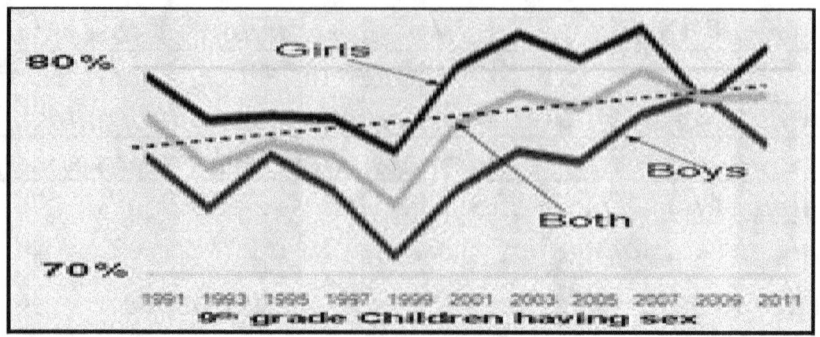

**Metro-Sexuality Rather Than Heterosexuality**- Innocent Ninth grade students at one northern California high school, and other locations, are learning more than just the birds and the bees as part of this Common Core destruction. Today we hear about something they call Metro-sexuality rather than hetero-sexuality. I know they sound the same, but they are soooo very different. Included in the materials provided to students about this metro sexuality were documents and worksheets that included a checklist entitled, *"Sex Check! Are You Ready For Sex?"* in which the 13 and 14-year-old students are asked questions such as-

- *Do they have water–based lubricants and condoms?*

- *Do they think they could handle a possible infection or pregnancy?*

Another worksheet reads like a how-to on obtaining consent from a possible sexual partner and offers possible statements like-

- *"Do you want to go back to my place?"*

- *"Is it OK if I take my pants off?"*

No time for science as our school is now turned into a sex-a-torium. The preoccupation of sex and its substantial increase has limited learning, caused a rift between our young children and the moral elements of our society. This may start with sex, but certainly we can see a correlation between this level of moral decay and illicit drug use. Both of these are heavy factors in enslaving our population.

# The Amendments

Before many of the delegates would consider the new Constitution, they wanted to ensure more States Rights so they insisted on a long list of "amendments" that would be added as soon as Congress had time to debate the words used in the Amendments. These would be known as the Bill of Rights. For completeness, I think we need to look at this first group of Amendments. It seems that a number of the Amendments that were established to convert the Constitution were not always focused on our country, but were, instead focused on some near-term incident and very poorly written. While I believe there are limitations, if changes to our laws are desired, they should necessarily be changed by Congress and not by the Supreme Court as it is a violation of all we hold dear concerning making a Constitution in the first place. We should at least look at a few to ensure they match up with the Constitution. Luckily or unluckily, we have government officials that misread the Amendments to make them say what they think they should say. I went over the illegal Amendments numbered 13, 13 number 2, 14, and 15, but there are some issues with the others that some seem to ignore. The first question might be how many amendments made up what is called the Bill of Rights? If you answered 10 you are well informed, but wrong. There were actually 12 Bill-of-Rights developed by Madison and passed through congress to finally be sent out to have 3/5 of the States ratification. Of the 12, 10 passed very quickly, but the 1st and second amendments had some issues. The copy of the Bill-of-Rights sent to the States for ratification in 1789 contained 12 amendments, which sounds as wrong as the Twelve Commandments. Originally, the First Amendment said that the number of seats in the House should grow with the population — a system that could have resulted in a 6,000-member Congress today. The Second Amendment dealt with Congressional pay, and was finally accepted some 200 years later as the 27th Amendment without having to have congress even vote on the thing as there was finally enough State's votes to have a $3/5^{th}$ majority and it became law. All 12 amendments as shown on the document below.

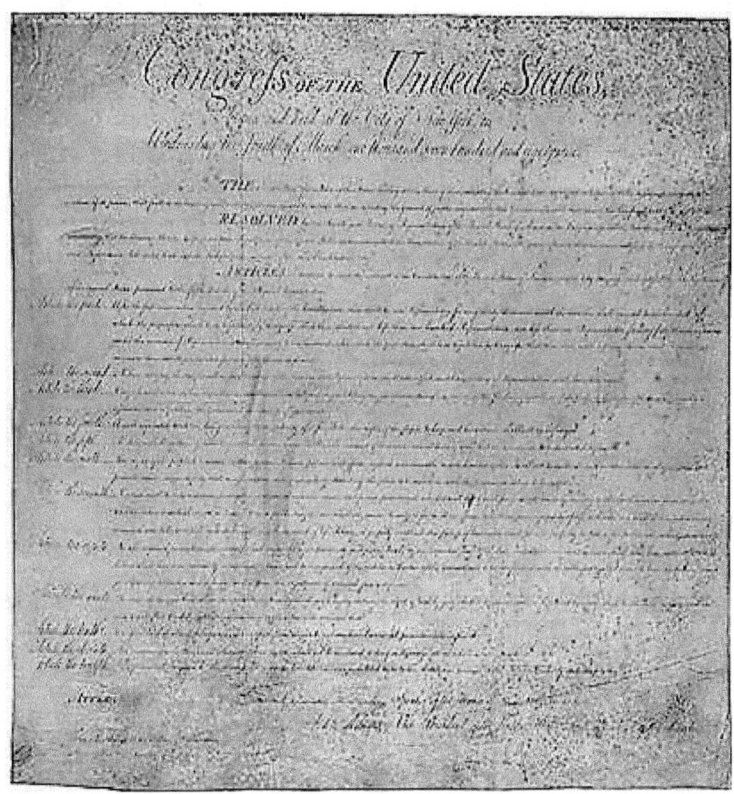

It is the 1st amendment we need to investigate before we get into the others. It seems that the original tally had the 2nd amendment with only 49% of the States in agreement, but the 1st amendment was different as 8 of the 14 States, 57% determined they wanted the amendment confirmed. Connecticut submitted it desire to have all 12 amendments pass a few weeks after the other 10 passed making it 64% in favor of the 1st amendment. This still was not enough, but he following year, Vermont became the 15th State and voted all 12 Amendments as acceptable. This made the vote 10 in favor and 5 against or 67%, making this the law of the land.

# First Amendment

Madison's original proposal for a bill of rights provision concerning religion read:

*"The civil rights of none shall be abridged on account of religious belief or worship, nor shall any national religion be established, nor shall the full and equal rights of conscience be in any manner, or on any pretense, infringed."*

The language was altered in the House to read: "Congress shall make no law establishing religion, or to prevent the free exercise thereof, or to infringe the rights of conscience. Finally, it was adopted as:

***Congress shall make no law*** *respecting an establishment of religion, or prohibiting the free exercise thereof;*

***Congress shall make no law*** *to limit the freedom of speech,*

***Congress shall make no law*** *to limit the freedom of the press,*

***Congress shall make no law*** *to limit the right of the people peaceably to assemble, and to petition the Government for a redress of grievances.*

> Wow! what a change! It is not known if the House readdressed this petition with all these changes, but notice *"Congress shall make no law that infringes of provided the pretense on the rights of conscience"* was removed.

**Freedom of Religion**-To eliminate this law, the Supreme court decided to change the definition of religion to take away God. Now something called secularism is considered a religion to be protected. As secularism says man is his own God, he would be the one giving himself inalienable rights that can overpower the government. In a different way of thinking these anti-God secularists cannot be allowed to have any inalienable rights as they have no God to give them to them.

**Limiting Freedom of Speech**- As implied by the first sentence, one cannot disparage God worshipped by another in that speech so speaking about eliminating the Ten Commandments or not allowing a shirt saying Christmas on it are not only violations of the religion part-it certainly is not allow under the second. This still allows for consequences for slander, inciting a riot, initiating insurrection and other key elements sometimes ignored.

**Limiting Freedom of the Press**- This still allows for consequences for slander, inciting a riot, initiating insurrection and other key elements sometimes ignored. This has nothing to do with protecting a source for something written. That is not found here. It was just made up and the Supreme Court, incorrectly made a law without Congress so it can be undone.

# Second Amendment

*A well-regulated Militia, being necessary to the security of a free State, the <u>right of the people to keep and bear Arms</u>, shall not be infringed.*

The idea of <u>bearing </u>rather than <u>having</u> is an interesting issue. It would seem that if you are allowed to "bear" arms against the State as implied by the Militia statement, there MUST be an allowance to HAVE THOSE ARMS---JUST IN CASE.

Somehow people have twisted this thing to say people cannot have powerful weapons because they could counter those of the police forces, but that is exactly what the Amendment was for. Some have suggested that a non-automatic AR15 was a combat weapon, but I will tell you no soldier would go against an enemy without the automatic feature of the M16. They cry out that our streets are too violent but instead of trying to remove the handguns that cause almost all killings, these people go after rifles that cannot be secretly brought into a place for nefarious reasons. There is not was our government can be allowed to take away our citizen's means to protect themselves from and abusive government---period.

# Third Amendment

*No Soldier shall, in time of peace be quartered in any house, without the consent of the Owner; <u>nor in time of war,</u> but in a manner to be prescribed by law.*

Here is where we must recognize, the Southern States were not allowed to secede so they were part of the United States and still Union soldiers took control of many homes of those who happened to live in the southern States of the "United States" outside of the constitutional law. This was exactly why this law was put in place and it failed when its meat was first tested during our 4th Civil War [1860-1865] but if we do not consider it a "Civil" War, the Agrarian States would not have this right. Somehow, people seem to forget this was supposedly a "Civil Action".

The last part is almost funny as the only way to allow quartering to be done is for it to be prescribed by law, but the representatives of all of the southern States were not allowed to vote so no law could be passed.

# Fourth Amendment

*The right of the people to be secure in their persons, houses, papers, and effects, against unreasonable searches and seizures, shall not be violated, and no Warrants shall issue, but upon probable cause, supported by Oath or affirmation, and particularly describing the place to be searched, and the persons or things to be seized.* While this makes absolutely no sense, some of the essence of how it has been used seems very good. Let's see what it does say!

This is simply saying ANY OATH OR AFFIRMATION [by anyone, including the person wanting to do the search] indicating where one will search is all that is needed to allow a search. ---Pretty stupid, but it is the law! How dare a judge not grant me the opportunity to search a place when I publicly describe where I am going to search!!!!!!

By the way! If you are wondering about the word "Warrant", here are the many definitions. One would expect that **any** would be allowed for the sentence, except the execution one. Any authorization; justification; guarantee; pledge; warehouse receipt; Any issuance by any magistrate authorizing arrest, seizure, search, or execution. *[Certainly, this is not talking about executions]*

As far as I know, no one has repurposed this amendment to make sense. It would be good to have it changed if we could get ¾ of the Congress to agree on anything.

# Fifth Amendment

**Part A-** This is actually 2 Amendments in one. This is the first part.

*No person shall be held to answer for a capital, or otherwise infamous crime, unless on a presentment or indictment of a Grand Jury, except in cases arising in the land or naval forces, or in the Militia, when in actual service in time of War or public danger.*

*No person shall be subject for the same offence to be twice put in jeopardy of life or limb.*

*No person shall be compelled in any "criminal case" to be a witness against himself.*

This is saying a Grand Jury must indict all capitol or horrible crime unless it is a military matter during a war or a military matter. One other method is if the crime was considered to be of public danger, whatever that means.

**The second part can be read to be pretty stupid.** *"If the offence is killing and you kill two people you can only be tried for killing one."* One can say killing the second person is a different type of crime, but it really is the same crime.

---

**The third part has been misused for years**… It is saying, *"A policeman cannot ask you direct questions that could have you testify against yourself.*, once you tell them what you did, they most likely will get one of those grand jury things going and then put you on trial where you can plead the 5th all you want to.*"

---

# Fifth Amendment [Part B]

*No person shall be deprived of life, liberty, or property, without due process of law; nor shall private property be taken for public use without just compensation.*

**Another stupid law!** How can anyone be killed in War as there is "no due process". In fact, no one can even tell you to go to war to kill someone. How can a criminal kill someone without "due process"? It is nonsensical. Some will try to tell you this is only talking about Americans, but it absolutely doesn't say that either.

**The second part is just as stupid**-----As far as the government taking your tax money from you without compensation, I don't have anything to say. I suppose the just compensation is that they won't rip you out of your home and put you in prison if you give them tax money, but that is a stretch.

# 6<sup>th</sup> & 7<sup>th</sup> Amendments

## Sixth Amendment

*In all criminal prosecutions, the accused shall enjoy the right to a speedy and public trial, by an impartial jury of the State and district wherein the crime shall have been committed; which district shall have been previously ascertained by law, and to be informed of the nature and cause of the accusation; to be confronted with the witnesses against him; to have **compulsory** process for obtaining witnesses in his favor; and to have the assistance of counsel for his defense.*

I hate to say it but this is a stupid law. It says a person cannot be on trial if there are no witnesses in his favor. I know some will say the word "process" simply you have to try, but a "Process that tries" to find a favorable witness is not the same as a process that finds a favorable witness.

## Seventh Amendment

*In Suits at common law, where the value in controversy shall exceed twenty dollars, the right of trial by jury shall be preserved, and no fact tried by a jury shall be otherwise reexamined in any Court of the United States, then according to the rules of common law.*

***This seems stupid as well.*** *What dictated common law and the idea that someone claiming to have lost 20 dollars' worth of anything and forcing a cost to the government of hundreds of dollars to find an acceptable jury is totally absurd.*

# 8th and 9th Amendments

## Eighth Amendment

Excessive bail shall not be required, nor excessive fines imposed, nor cruel and unusual punishments inflicted.

**Seems like a reasonable law! [Finally!]**

## Ninth Amendment

*The enumeration in the Constitution of certain rights shall not be construed to deny or disparage others retained by the people.*

**This is nonsensical**. If someone feels they have the right to kill someone, but the Constitution says you should not do it, we should not disparage his right to feel that way.

**Some have twisted this one around** to say anything not explicitly identified in the Constitution is a right retained by an individual. If the Constitution doesn't specifically say starving a person until they die is bad, one can do that because it is the lack of food killing him not the person.

# Tenth Amendment

*The powers not delegated to the United States by the Constitution, nor prohibited by it to the States, are reserved to the States respectively, **or to the people**.*

**Some have claimed the *"or the people"* part is to be ignored** as it makes the law stupid. Yes, it does; but changing the law is not allowed without Congress. Essentially it is saying that State Law is not binding as the Constitution claims the State and the Person are equal on anything not in the Constitution.

That being said, the ONLY things delegated to the United States government are the following:
- To lay and collect Taxes
- To pay for the common Defense and general Welfare
- To borrow Money on the credit of the United States
- To regulate Commerce with foreign Nations
- To establish Rule of Naturalization and Bankruptcy
- To coin Money and regulate the Value
- To provide for the Punishment of counterfeiting;
- To establish Post Offices;
- To promote the Progress of Science and useful Arts,
- To constitute Tribunals inferior to the supreme Court;
- To define and punish Pirates;
- To declare War;
- To raise and support an Army for no longer than two Years;
- To provide and maintain a Navy;

- To make Rules for land and naval Forces;
- To execute the Laws of the Union and repel Invasions;
- To organize and train the Militia
- To control less than 10 miles of State lands [if the State allows] for Forts and other needful Buildings
- To make Laws for the above items <u>ONLY</u>.
- To define who is allowed to accept money, Office, or Title, from any King, Prince, or foreign State.
- To determine and collect all Duties on Imports or Exports,
- To Determine and collect Duty of Tonnage, keep Troops, or Ships of War in time of Peace, enter into any Agreement with a foreign Power

# 11<sup>th</sup> Amendments

### The First Eleventh Amendment [1789]

Let's reads it. It's almost funny that we simply ignore Constitutional Amendments like the first 13<sup>th</sup> amendment and this one.

*After the first enumeration required by the first article of the Constitution, there shall be one Representative for every thirty thousand, until the number shall amount to one hundred, after which the proportion shall be so regulated by Congress, that there shall be not less than one hundred Representatives, nor less than one Representative for every forty thousand persons, until the number of Representatives shall amount to two hundred; after which the proportion shall be so regulated by Congress, that there shall not be less than two hundred Representatives, nor more than one Representative for every fifty thousand persons.*

### Crazy Law That is not Followed

As I stated this would require the Congress to have grown to 6000 people so that a congressman for each 50 thousand would be represented. While one might think this may have reduced the unequal representation of Congress with respect to the tiny Statettes associated with New England it probably would not have nor would it have halted the 4<sup>th</sup> Civil War. Because Connecticut submitted later, the vote simply wasn't taken and over time, no one registered the

Connecticut vote, until now. What a dilemma. Just like the Prohibition war and the anti-prohibition law that had to be used to erase it, this one will have to be erased by another amendment. Such is the life of our 3rd Constitution. The remaining "normal"10 bill of rights were written in a horrible way allowing for reasonable interpretation to go towards the absurd as well. Let's see what they say.

## The Second Eleventh Amendment [1794]

*The Judicial power of the United States **shall not** be construed to extend to any suit in law or equity, commenced or prosecuted against one of the United States by Citizens of another State, or by Citizens or Subjects of any Foreign State.*

This simply modifies Article III, section 2, of the Constitution.

# Twelfth Amendment [1804]

*The Electors shall meet in their respective states and vote by ballot for President and Vice-President, one of whom, at least, shall not be an inhabitant of the same state with themselves; they shall name in their ballots the person voted for as President, and in distinct ballots the person voted for as Vice-President, and they shall make distinct lists of all persons voted for as President, and of all persons voted for as Vice-President, and of the number of votes for each, which lists they shall sign and certify, and transmit sealed to the seat of the government of the United States, directed to the President of the Senate; -- the President of the Senate shall, in the presence of the Senate and House of Representatives, open all the certificates and the votes shall then be counted; -- The person having the greatest number of votes for President, shall be the President, if such number be a majority of the whole number of Electors appointed; and if no person have such majority, then from the persons having the highest numbers not exceeding three on the list of those voted for as President, the House of Representatives shall choose immediately, by ballot, the President. But in choosing the President, the votes shall be taken by states, the representation from each state having one vote; a quorum for this purpose shall consist of a member or members from two-thirds of the states and a majority of all the states shall be necessary to a choice. [And if the House of Representatives shall not choose a*

*President whenever the right of choice shall devolve upon them, before the fourth day of March next following, then the Vice-President shall act as President, as in case of the death or other constitutional disability of the President. --]\* The person having the greatest number of votes as Vice-President, shall be the Vice-President, if such number be a majority of the whole number of Electors appointed, and if no person have a majority, then from the two highest numbers on the list, the Senate shall choose the Vice-President; a quorum for the purpose shall consist of two-thirds of the whole number of Senators, and a majority of the whole number shall be necessary to a choice. But no person constitutionally ineligible to the office of President shall be eligible to that of Vice-President of the United States.*

This amendment suspended Article II, section 1 of the Constitution. They found out this was no good either so they came up with the 20th Amendment later. Vice President Jefferson was the only one ever elected by this bad method.

# 13th Amendments

There were 2 of these. One before the Civil War and one after the war. The first one gave States the total right to hold on to the custom of Slavery while the second one, removed Slavery as soon as the government paid for the slaves in the North.

## The 1st 13ᵗʰ Amendment [1860]

Initially proposed by Representative Thomas Corwin of Ohio, this proslavery bill was initiated <u>while the southern members were leaving the assembly</u>. Surely, the bill would be thrown out without the southern States to vote for it. Instead, <u>the amendment passed the House as Joint Resolution No. 80 on February 28 by a landslide vote of **133 to 65,**</u> which was two-thirds of the members present as <u>the southern congressmen had all left</u>. It didn't stop there either. On March 2, the Senate acted in favor of the proposed amendment by a vote of **24 to 12** and President Buchanan signed the joint resolution the day the Senate approved it. The new law would become a constitutional amendment as soon as it was ratified by the States. Two States, Ohio and Maryland ratified it right away and others might have followed except for a peculiar war that had begun. Signed by Buchanan, <u>This Amendment was pushed by an old friend named Abraham Lincoln. Because of Lincoln's efforts, it almost became the law of the land.</u> Abraham Lincoln sent personal letters to urge the signing of this amendment that would keep federal law away from Slavery. The graphic shows one of the letters sent to Florida.

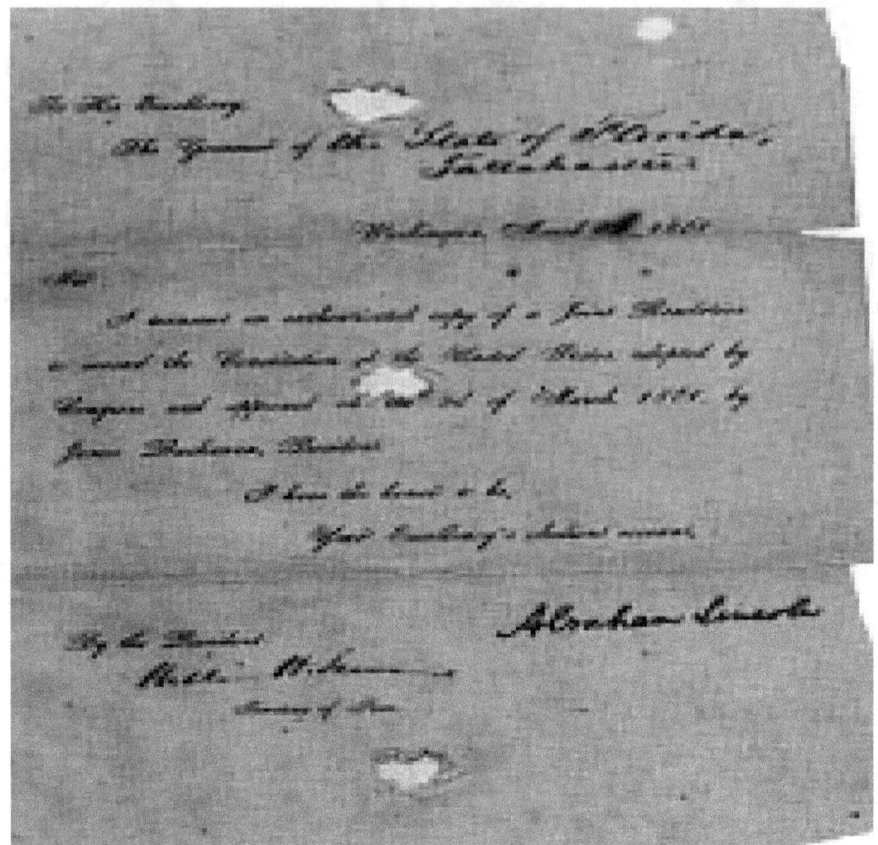

## What Corwin & Lincoln Had Pushed Through

Below is a portion of the proposed 13th amendment Lincoln supported push for. This is the amendment that both the Senate and House of Representatives had agreed was best for the country.

*"No amendment shall be made to the Constitution which will authorize or give to Congress the power to abolish or interfere, within any State, with the domestic institutions thereof, including that of persons held to labor or service by the laws of said State."*

> *In other words, "Slaves are fine if a State says they are fine. The federal government will not interfere."*

It would have effectively made slavery untouchable by any future constitutional amendment; thereby preventing at any time in the future what became the second 13th amendment. It would have prolonged the existence of slavery where it existed beyond a possible future abolition by peaceful means and Lincoln was one of its strong supporters.

> *With this amendment getting so much support, aren't you wondering how the whole country turned around in just a couple of months and were willing to allow 600 thousand men to die for what this amendment was trying to protect.*

## 2nd 13th Amendment [1865]

Let's call this one the "Now that the USA has Bought the Northern Slaves we Can't Have Slaves" Law. I already discussed this briefly, but the Amendment is very simple and very simply stated.

> *There can be no involuntary Servitude or slavery.*
> *[except Chinese]*

Even after this one passed, the United States still was in process of paying money, ILLEGALY, to slave owners to buy their slaves. Technically, the United States had finished making payment for the slaves, but the final dollars were paid after it was against the law. It should have read, "No slaves are allowed unless you have some. If you do, the United States will buy them from you because you are not doing anything wrong. O yeah! States that fought on the side of the Agrarian States, even though we are one country again, will not get any payment just because." If the United States is still in process of buying my slaves, they will continue to pay me even though the transfer is now considered illegal."

*Neither slavery nor involuntary servitude, except as a punishment for crime whereof the party shall have been duly convicted, shall exist within the United States, or any place subject to their jurisdiction. Congress shall have power to enforce this article by appropriate legislation.*

As I explained this was to suspend Article IV, section 2, of the Constitution and it was initiated with only a few Congressmen as it was **totally adopted against the law**. This law did not give Chinese any rights so it is very odd.

# Fourteenth Amendment [1868]

***Section 1- Anti-Slavery except Chinese Law-****All persons born or naturalized in the United States, and subject to the jurisdiction thereof, are citizens of the United States and of the State wherein they reside. No State shall make or enforce any law which shall abridge the privileges or immunities of citizens of the United States; nor shall any State deprive any person of life, liberty, or property, without due process of law; nor deny to any person within its jurisdiction the equal protection of the laws.*

***Section2- The Southerners and Indians Aren't Americans Law-****Representatives shall be apportioned among the several States according to their respective numbers, counting the whole number of persons in each State, excluding Indians not taxed. But when the right to vote at any election for the choice of electors for President and Vice-President of the United States, Representatives in Congress, the Executive and Judicial officers of a State, or the members of the Legislature thereof, is denied to any of the male inhabitants of such State, being twenty-one years of age,\* and citizens of the United States, or in any way abridged, except for participation in rebellion, or other crime, the basis of representation therein shall be reduced in the proportion which the number of such **male citizens***

*shall bear to the whole number of **male citizens twenty-one** years of age in such State.*

**Section 3 ---People of the south should not have rights to vote on or hold public office law-** *No person shall be a Senator or Representative in Congress, or elector of President and Vice-President, or hold any office, civil or military, under the United States, or under any State, who, having previously taken an oath, as a member of Congress, or as an officer of the United States, or as a member of any State legislature, or as an executive or judicial officer of any State, to support the Constitution of the United States, shall have engaged in insurrection or rebellion against the same, or given aid or comfort to the enemies thereof. But Congress may by a vote of two-thirds of each House, remove such disability.*

**Section 4. Only northerners would be paid for slaves' law-**The validity of the public debt of the United States, authorized by law, including debts incurred for payment of pensions and bounties for services in suppressing insurrection or rebellion, shall not be questioned. But neither the United States <u>nor any State shall assume or pay any debt or obligation incurred in aid of insurrection or rebellion against the United States, or any claim for the loss or emancipation of any slave</u>; but all such debts, obligations and claims shall be held illegal and void. The Congress shall have the power to enforce, by appropriate legislation, the provisions of this article.

This Amendment modified Article I, section 2, of the Constitution and a portion was changes by the 26<sup>th</sup>

Amendment, but Like the 13th, this one was ratified in a process that was not legal.

## The Agrarian State Humans-Aren't-Americans Law

In June of 1866, the Fourteenth Amendment to the Constitution was proposed to the States for adoption and finally adopted in 1868. This "Grant Law" really was enacted to ensure that the mock representatives could continue for a long time. Hidden in the Amendment was the following:

*Section 2-No person should hold office under United States authority, who, had aided or engaged in the war against the Union. It also enforced the repudiation of all debts or obligations "incurred in the aid of insurrection or rebellion against the United States."*

Luckily, none of the people who were affected were considered citizens anyway so they could not vote against this great law. By the way, the law was passed and then 3 impossibly strange things occurred.

- *THE LAW BECAME RETROACTIVE,*
- *ONLY AFFECTED THE CIVIL WAR PARTICIPANTS,*
- *AND HAS NEVER BEEN USED AGAINST ANY OTHER GROUP.*

*Weird isn't it? How can you change the Constitution and then say, "Oh yeah! We really made this change in the Constitution 8 years ago. We have passed this Constitutional "Change" and the congress years earlier would have approved it. TRUST US!!*

PLEASE REMEMBER!!! THIS LAW WAS MADE MANY YEARS AFTER THE WAR HAD ENDED, SO IT CANNOT MAKE SENSE. How can teachers across the country teach about constitutional law, come upon this thing, know [or should know] about how it was used during the reformation, and give it a place with NORMAL laws.

Here is the essence of the Amendment.

- *Anyone who aided an insurrection against the U.S. cannot hold office or ever be complete citizens.*
- *If citizens were part of any previous insurrection, then they will not be counted among citizens when establishing numbers of legislators. [Even a slave was worth 3/5 of a person but the huge group of non-slave survivors were considered to be 0% of a person]*
- *Indians shall not be taxed [This doesn't seem like the same law, but they stuck it in anyway.]*
- *The United States will not compensate Americans for loss of slaves. [Well, well; --there wasn't any more because the government already compensated everyone.]*

For those thinking this was such a great law what it really said was the following:

*Until everyone was dead that lived during the 4th Civil War, no representation was assured in the south. Sometimes you've got to admire the insight of the ~~American~~ New England Congress.*

This one insured that no representation from the Southern States was even possible. It became against the Law to be a representative of the Agrarian States who had now been back as part of the country for the last 5 years. Because no one that even helped the Agrarian States was allowed in Congress, many States like Virginia, Georgia, Florida, North and South Carolina, Alabama, and Arkansas thought this was a great law and <u>THEIR REPRESENTATIVES voted for it</u>.

Delaware rejected the new Law, but here is a kicker, 30 years later the Statette ratified it. If you think that is strange, California and Oregon didn't ratify the Law for 90 years afterwards. Additionally, Kentucky, Maryland, and Tennessee have continued to indicate that this illegal law is a terrible one. I think that the last three are the only sane ones.

I'm certainly not against the Constitution of the United States, but this particular illegal law is SO TERRIBLE, that someone-----ANYONE should address it, reevaluate it, remove it and destroy all memory of it.

## Oddity

Here is another one of those strange things. Notice the part number 4. <u>In 1865, they passed a law against slavery, but it wasn't until 1868 that the United States had to stop paying slave owners for their slaves. Something sounds fishy to me and it is NEVER addressed in our schools.</u>

## How Stupid Can a Law Be?

Let's just look at the words "any previous insurrection". We would have to count the American Revolution Insurrection, Shay's Civil War, the Whiskey Tax Civil War, and Bloody Kansas Civil War. If all the founding fathers were not allowed to be in Congress, there is no Constitution to worry about in the first place. By this stupid law there is NO QUESTION. We have no Constitution, until a new one is made that had no people previously in an insurrection. I'm sure the New Englander's hated this law as it gave them even more power.

# Fifteenth Amendment
# [1870]

This is the Black right to vote, but it still excluded Chinese slaves held by the Railroad companies.

**Section 1-** *The right of citizens of the United States to vote shall not be denied or abridged by the United States or by any State on account of race, color, or previous condition of servitude-- The Congress shall have the power to enforce this article by appropriate legislation.*

Like the preceding 2 Amendments that are bogus, but this one is even boguser as Chinese were not allowed to vote even after this ratification.

*"All Races and colors have the right to vote, if they are considered citizens." [This excluded Chinese of course who were denied citizenship and much more.]*

Unlike its predecessor, this is a great law. It would have been better if it included Chinese right away.

Unfortunately, it also has been greatly misrepresented. It was not passed because people wanted freed slaves to vote to make up for some previous injustice, but rather, most of the white voters were not allowed to vote and this LAW allowed unscrupulous industrialist State "lobbyists" to buy votes from the very small minority of uneducated

Southerners so that agrarian power would be eliminated. Some of you will not believe this no matter what evidence is provided, but, at least, keep an open mind of this possibility. I'm sure that the 13th and 15th amendments would pass if presented again, but right now there is serious question concerning the validity of these laws and instructors don't seem to talk about these things in our High Schools and Colleges. I'm sorry I spent so much time on these things, but they were so despicable, that the laws and amendments passed during that time should be stricken and re-voted on to make them have some semblance of legality.

### Drinking Laws [18 and 21]

Besides not allowing Ice Cream to be sold on Sunday which made the Sundae [Ice Cream with Syrup a big hit, the Drinking laws actually increased drinking and violence associated with it.

### Eighteenth Amendment [1919]

The others are fairly mundane except for the 18th, of course. This is the prohibition law.

### 21st Amendment [1933]

The 21st Amendment eliminated it in 1933.

# Conclusions

I am sure I got many people angry on both sides of current debates on governing styles, but please understand there is a huge risk of our country dying if we don't do something drastic.

- We must get back to the principles of the 3$^{rd}$ Constitution or we will have nothing soon enough.

- We must put restrictions and controls on industry to limit monopoly or we will die.

- We must halt the slavery of the poor by giving payment for not working and punishment for working.

- We must revamp our schools and replace free spirit with discipline.

- We must replace coddling of the disruptive students with praise for those working hard.

- We must put emphasis on learning and reduce the importance of being a basketball star.

- We must immediately halt the destruction of children's morals in the name of helping them be comfortable with their own bodies.

- We must halt the continuing acceptance of deviations to focus on normalcy

- We must limit payment for mistake to reasonable effect.

- We must put controls on the AMA and the cost of medicine to be regulated by common cost around the world.

- We must instill patriotism and not be afraid to require American ideals and language if people wish to stay in our country.

- We must reduce the huge number of illegal aliens sucking the life out of America just like Hoover and Eisenhower did.

- We must instill the words of John F. Kennedy, *"It is not what the country can do for you but what YOU CAN DO FOR THE COUNTRY"*, so quickly erased by Lynden Johnson.

We cannot survive as a fascist or communist State and a democracy will always fail. The only acceptable government in a wealthy nation is a REPUBLIC. Our constitution allows for it and our descendants need it desperately.

# About the Author

Steve Preston is a long lime author of scientific, esoteric facts. His books focus on the painful truths rather than whitewashed details that make us comfortable. If you are interested in the truth instead of comfort, please review other works by Mr. Preston as shown below. The images are some from Egypt on the left. To the right the writer is shown with his investigative friends in the Jewish Negev desert of Israel where the Dead Sea Scrolls were found that were used by John the Baptist in his Essene-like teachings.

Other investigations are also shown. To the left below are a couple of pictures as we searched the New Zealand caves possibly visited by the ancient Maori and the last image is of the author investigating the statues on the Acropolis in Athens Greece.

A list of most of my books are listed next. Besides this last group on time-travel, his books include a wide assortment of different subjects including Biblical History and proofs, the story of man's development, ancient tecnology, new views of physics and biology, ancient wars, current fears and events. A partial list follows:

## *Development of Mankind*
*The First Creation of Man-book 1 History of mankind*
*The Second Creation of Man-book 2 History of mankind*
*The Creation of Adam and Eve-book 3 History of mankind*
*The Antediluvian War Years-book 4 History of mankind*
*Man After The Flood-book 5 History of mankind*
*A Closer Look at Ancient History-book 6 History of mankind*
*A New View of Modern History-book 7 History of mankind*
*The Twentieth Century and Beyond- book 8 History of Mankind*

## *Biblical History*
*Adam's First Wife-Story of Lilith*
*Incarnations of God- How often did God become Incarnated?*
*History Confirmed By The Bible- Science confirmation of the Bible*
*Moses Saved Egypt- How the Jews eliminated the Hyksos*
*Mysteries of the Exodus- Proofs of the Exodus*
*Why the King James Bible Failed- Issues with KJB*

## *Bible Analysis*
*Abraham to Moses-First part of the Bible*
*Adam to Abraham- Second Part of the Bible*
*Moses to Jesus- Third part of the Bible Series*
*Understanding the New Testament-4$^{th}$ part of the Bible Series*
*Closer Look At Genesis- 200 ancient text confirm Genesis*
*Exploring Exodus- Reviewing the Details of "Exodus"*
*Errors in Understanding- Interpretations of the Bible*
*Expanded Genesis- Apocrypha and other Jewish texts*
*New look at the Bible- Questions in Interpretation*
*Old Testament Used By Jesus- Ancient Jewish texts*
*Exploring Genesis- Reviewing the details of "Genesis'*

## *Ancient Technology and Life*
*Amazing Technology- Pleistocene Technology*

*Nephilimic Gods- History of the Ancient Giant/gods*
*Ancient History of Flying- Ancient flying*
*Kingdoms Before the Flood- Pleistocene humans*
*Living on Venus- Venus before the Pleistocene Extinction*
*Martians- Ancient Life on Mars*
*Mysterious Pyramids- Who made the Pyramids?*
*Victory of the Earth- History of our Earth*
*Not from Space- UFOs are not from space.*
*Space Anomalies-Anomalies and Analysis of space*
*Secrets of Thoth- Analysis of the 7 tablets of Thoth*
*Amazing Technology- Descriptions of prehistoric capabilities*

**Ancient and Modern War**
*America's Civil War Lie- Truth about the Civil War years*
*Behind the Tower of Babel- Story of the Bharata War*
*Driven Underground- Fear in the Bharata War*
*Four Armageddons- The 4 major wars that destroyed mankind*
*Six Deaths of Man- Destructions of mankind*
*World War Before- The Pleistocene War*
*World War with Heaven- The Angel and Nephilim War*
*World War Zero-The Bharata War*
*When Giants Ruled the Earth- History of the Titan Giants*
*Sex Crazed Angels- What caused the Heaven War?*

**Current Events and Fears**
*Allah' God of the Moon- Terror of Muslims*
*American School Disaster- fear in our country*
*Can We Save America? - Fear in the USA*
*Scythians Conquer Ireland- A History of Ireland*
*Fast History of MILES Training- Laser based Army training*
*Great American Quiz- Unusual details of American History*
*Make Your Own Global Warming-Tricks that look like warming*
*Modern Misconception- Misconceptions in Science*
*Truth About Phoenicia- The Evidence -First in America*
*Monsters are Alive- Post Pleistocene Monsters*
*Promote the General Welfare- Fear in USA*
*Our Very Odd Presidents- President review*
*Terror of Global Warming- Fake issue uncovered*

*The Antichrist- Many demonic possessed rulers*
*The Bad Side of Lincoln- Negative side of a great man*
*The Devil- Of Demons and their master*
*Vampires among Us- How Demons and Vampires are similar*
*Humans on Display- Slavery and Human Zoos*
*Romans Found America- American Trade before Columbus*

**New Look at Physics**
*Anthropic Reality- We control our Reality*
*Consensus Science- Fake Science*
*Complex Earth- Truth behind Earth's development*
*Is Time Travel Possible? Science of Time Travel*
*Retiming the Earth- Eliminate of Nuclear Decay Errors*
*Releasing Your Consciousness- Beyond our SELF*
*Slip Through a Wall- How to walk through solids*
*Our 12-Dimensional Universe- New science of our Universe*
*Mystery of Photons and Light- Science of Photons*
*Of Heaven and Hell- scientific descriptions*
*Meaning of Life and Light- Detains of New Science*
*Vibrational Matter- New Science of Quantum Fluctuations*
*Incredible Tesla- Examination of his discoveries*
*Death Without Death-The Life of one's Soul*

**New Look at Biology**
*Understand Your Heart- New discoveries of the Heart Brain*
*DNA of Our Ancestors- Tracing DNA of ancient man*
*God Didn't Make The Ape- New science on ape Evolution*
*Lizard People- Mutated People of the Bharata War*
*Creation and Death of Dinosaurs- Why Dinosaurs died*
*Races of Men- Tracing DNA of Humans*
*Tracing Cro-Magnon to Jesus- The third creation and mutation*
*Self, Soul, Spirit- Three components of Life*
*Self-Virtualization- New science of reality*
*True Happiness- Self Actualism and Beyond*
*Life Resonance- Unusual capabilities of men*
*Awaken the Departed- We can talk to the Dead*
*Biophotonics and Healing- How Photonics used in medicine*

***Time Traveling Empath Historical Fiction***
*Conrad and the Flood- James aids survivors of the Pleistocene Extinction*
*Shama and the Tower- James aids the survival of India during the Aryan Invasion*
*Naille and the Exodus- James aids the survival of Jews & Scythians of the Exodus*
*Secrets of Washington- James insures Washington become President*

www.ingramcontent.com/pod-product-compliance
Lightning Source LLC
Chambersburg PA
CBHW071341280526
45787CB00001B/177